What people are sa

Fairy – The Otherworld l

Finally! I have been waiting for a book like this for years. Morgan Daimler has done it again, taking an often difficult to approach subject matter and making it both accessible and enticing. In *Fairy – The Otherworld by Many Names* we are essentially taken on a whistlestop tour of various Otherworldly lands found throughout lore from the Celtic nations. Providing the reader with essential foundational information in a clear and concise manner, this book is the perfect primer or spring board for building a deeper understanding of the land of Fairy. Part the mists, come under the mound, and find yourself lost in the enchantment of this book! A must read for anyone with an interest in fairy lore, Celtic myths, or all things unearthly!

Mhara Starling, author of *Welsh Witchcraft: A Guide to the Spirits, Lore, and Magic of Wales*

Morgan Daimler invites us on a spectacular journey to the Otherworld. She vividly presents a host of helpful information that both allow the reader to understand what can be a contradictory subject and to come to their own conclusions as well. This is a marvelous work of scholarship that should be primary for anyone looking to explore the realm of Fairy and know its inhabitants. Morgan's work once again shows us why she is the preeminent expert on all things Fairy related in the modern era.

Mark NeCamp, Jr., author of *Energy Magick*

The Otherworld is an elusive place of magick and mysterious beings. There have been many strange tales of this place where the fairies call home. In her new book, *Fairy*, Morgan Daimler helps us peer through the mists of the Otherworld so that we may better connect to this magical place. Using folklore, story, and even pop culture, Daimler teaches us the many ways the world of Fairy has been seen over hundreds of years. This book is a wonderful guide for those who wish to dare tread into the world of the fairies.

Chris Allaun, author of *Otherworld: Ecstatic Witchcraft for the Spirits of the Land*

A concise exploration of the Celtic fairy realms, based on the most reliable extant sources from Ireland and Britain. It goes a long way to clearing up the immense confusion and inaccuracy on this subject – one that has rapidly regained popularity in the last few decades. The final section on contact with fairy wisely urges caution and respect, and rightly so, something that many lesser books gloss over, or omit entirely. This book may prove an invaluable guide to those interested in fairies, but who lack the knowledge or experience to engage with the subject in a meaningful way – Morgan Daimler has done all the hard work for you, all one need do is read and absorb the lessons herein.

Luke Eastwood, author of *The Druid's Primer, Samhain: The Roots of Halloween* & *Kerry Folk Tales*

Morgan has done the impossible in this book, which is to make some sense of the vastness of the Otherworlds. This is a comprehensive source that pulls from various separate, but connected, cultures to form a picture of the Otherworld that is clear enough to understand how we can never fully grasp it. I wish I had had this resource when I was in graduate school.

Blythe Rymer, author of *The Raven and the Lotus* blog

Drawing on Insular Celts and related cultures, Daimler offers a scholarly but accessible view on what people thought, and think, about the Otherworld, access to it, and its denizens. They are careful not to privilege some ideas over others, nor to confuse human beliefs and opinions about the Otherworld with the Otherworld itself. They also reveal how cultural ideas get informed by Christian ideas and the role of later literature particularly in the English material. Brief but full of food for thought, this book brings together rich original source material and contradictory conceptions to give a fulsome view of how we have understood the Otherworld and perhaps an oblique view of that place itself. I was delighted by the whole book, but especially the last chapter concerning beliefs regarding how to get in and, perhaps more importantly, how to get out of Fariy. This is an excellent overview for anyone interested in fairies and their realm and I highly recommend it.

Brian Walsh, author of *The Secret Commonwealth and the Fairy Belief Complex*

Fairy is a fascinating study that examines beliefs in Fairy – the magical world – from across Celtic languages speaking cultures. The book is complex yet non-intimidating, with content clearly structured and accessible to a broad audience. Lore that is authentic to Celtic languages speaking cultures, scholarly research, and personal thought weave together to convey a fuller picture of Fairy, a picture that shows not just the mystery and magic but also that things coming down crashing when humans act poorly because of either ignorance or disregard for rules. *Fairy – The Celtic Otherworld By Many Names* is a must read for anyone interested to understand fairies and the importance of balance between their world and ours.

Daniela Simina, author of *Where Fairies Meet: Parallels between Irish and Romanian Fairy Traditions*, and *A Fairy Path: The Memoir of a Young Fairy Seer in Training*

Fairy

The Otherworld
by Many Names

Fairy

The Otherworld
by Many Names

Morgan Daimler

**MOON
BOOKS**

Winchester, UK
Washington, USA

JOHN HUNT PUBLISHING

First published by Moon Books, 2024
Moon Books is an imprint of John Hunt Publishing Ltd., No. 3 East Street, Alresford
Hampshire SO24 9EE, UK
office@jhpbooks.net
www.johnhuntpublishing.com
www.moon-books.net

For distributor details and how to order please visit the 'Ordering' section on our website.

Text copyright: Morgan Daimler 2023

ISBN: 978 1 78904 860 5
978 1 78904 861 2 (ebook)
Library of Congress Control Number: 2023932249

A CIP catalogue record for this book is available from the British Library.

Design: Lapiz Digital Services

UK: Printed and bound by CPI Group (UK) Ltd, Croydon, CR0 4YY
Printed in North America by CPI GPS partners

We operate a distinctive and ethical publishing philosophy in
all areas of our business, from our global network of authors to
production and worldwide distribution.

Contents

This book is dedicated to my friend Éilís. Your friendship meant the world to me when we were growing up and there are so many things that I was introduced to because of you, from Mercedes Lackey to the SCA. I can never thank you enough for all of the good memories.

With thanks to Trevor Greenfield for all your hard work and encouragement. I wouldn't be the author I am today without you.

Author's Note

This book is the result of many years of personal experience which led me to research the folklore and mythology surrounding the Western European belief in the world of Fairy. This subject has been one that I have felt a great deal of passion about as well as a consuming interest, and in writing this I am trying to share what I have found and learned with everyone who reads it.

Within the text I will be focusing on Otherworld beliefs from Ireland, Scotland, Wales, England, and modern popular culture. I would very much have liked to include places like the Isle of Man or Cornwall but found the sources for such lacking; I hope one day these beliefs are more available to the wider public. I also chose not to include Norse beliefs around Alfheim, despite the fact that these beliefs undoubtedly impacted at least Scottish folklore, because I wanted to keep the focus here as tight as possible and was worried that including the Norse would per force require casting a wider net in general than would serve the purpose here. Hopefully this tighter focus will be successful in conveying the beliefs in a cohesive and understandable fashion, but it is worth saying that the subject is even more complex than, and the beliefs more widespread, than I cover. This is a topic that a person can spend a lifetime studying and still not completely understand.

Every book ultimately reflects the biases of the author and for me Fairy is a real place that humans may interact with and which is the home of many different beings that may come into the human world. This view undoubtedly colours my opinions but I have done my best to be objective in what is shared here. I want everyone, no matter what your viewpoints are, to find some value in this book.

I personally favour using APA citation in my writing and so, throughout this book when a source is being cited, you will see the name of the author and date of the book in parenthesis after the sentence. I have also included end notes expanding on points that don't fit neatly into the larger text but are important to touch on. I strongly encourage people interested in going further with this subject to read the sources listed in the bibliography for themselves.

I hope that this book can serve as a good introduction for readers across any experience level to understand the convoluted beliefs around the world of Fairy, how that world has been understood across cultures which shared a belief in it, and how the perception of Fairy has changed across cultures and time.

Foreword

By Daniela Simina

Elusive and alluring like its own inhabitants, Fairy – the Celtic Otherworld – has fascinated humans since the oldest of times. Minds tried to make sense of what the eyes had seen and what senses sampled in those rare occasions when people stumbled into Fairy. Its location has become a torturous paradox for many. Is it real, and if so, then where exactly is it located? Is it regional? How is Fairy run, and why does human experience with it span such a broad spectrum, from blissfully rewarding to outright disastrous? Questions continue to arise. Debates have gone on centuries now, because who can claim to have definite answers?

Morgan Daimler's *Fairy: The Celtic Otherworld by Many Names* shines light on the sinuous path to Fairy and on the relevance of its interacting with the human world. The book is an invaluable resource for both scholars and lay people who seek to understand Fairy and connect with it. For the academically-oriented mind Fairy is the gift of exceptional scholarship. For the spiritual seeker it is a practical must-read. Fairy lore spanning centuries, brings to the reader's attention many instances of human – Fairy interaction and culture-specific beliefs about its location. Since such interactions do not exclusively belong to the past, gaining an understanding of Fairy is all the more important.

Fairy: The Celtic Otherworld by Many Names is a manifesto that raises awareness to the dangers of painting Fairy and fairies with exceedingly wide brushes, stripping them of individuality, and sweetening their looks and characters to suit certain tastes. Fairy lore acts as an intergenerational compass. Thus, distortion of older meanings and sweeping under the rug truths that are uncomfortable to a dominant culture – whether political, social

3

or religious colonialism – damage the compass. This book is an instrument for calibration through finding balance between the oldest and the newer views, and by understanding how social changes and religious ideas influence fairy lore of their time. In their approach, Morgan Daimler does not force onto readers a complete picture, but rather helps them develop one of their own; Fairy can be so many different things for different people.

Learning about the places which fairies inhabit adds substance to beliefs in their existence. Besides, this kind of knowledge is of practical use to those seeking to interact with them. To this avail, Morgan Daimler tackles the important yet oftentimes overlooked aspect of the proximity between human world and Fairy. From the older lore the emerging image is that of close, contingent worlds. The way human protagonists describe their inadvertent slipping into it or purposefully traveling there conveys the sense Fairy's closeness to the human world. In stark contrast to this more primary belief, the sharp dichotomy between human world and Fairy is the product of more recent influences which this book analyses. The implications of viewing the human world and Fairy as proximal instead of remote reverberates at all levels: social, cultural, and environmental. Viewing Fairy as intangible, as only existing on an "astral plane" leads to placing excessive value on the "spiritual", the immaterial, the distant Other, while treating consensus reality with entitlement and disrespect. Separation from Fairy breeds a mentality that gives license to all kinds of abuses toward the Earth and its inhabitants. For this reason, educating oneself about Fairy, the Celtic Otherworld, is of utmost importance today more than ever before.

In writing *Fairy: The Celtic Otherworld by Many Names*, Morgan Daimler places their wisdom and expertise in service to others and to the Other. As it is the case with their entire work, the contents of this book are not mere abstractions, and theoretical aspects never appear divorced from practical ones.

Fairy is a vehicle by which the author delivers sound knowledge and advice to those among us who are never happy to explore Fairy only as an intellectual exercise.

A practical tool and a precious gift, Morgan Daimler's *Fairy: The Celtic Otherworld by Many Names* guides the reader through the crossroads of dream and desire, fantasy and reality, all the way to Fairy and back.

Daniela Simina, author of *Where Fairies Meet: Parallels between Irish and Romanian Fairy Traditions*, and *A Fairy Path: The Memoir of a Young Fairy Seer in Training*

Introduction

And see not ye that bonny road,
That winds about the fernie brae?
That is the road to fair Elfland,
Where thou and I this night maun gae.
Thomas the Rhymer

Throughout history the land of Fairy, by any name, and its
inhabitants have fascinated and sometimes terrified humans,
appearing across western European cultures and across
centuries in literature and folklore and personal anecdotes.[1]
There is something both enchanting and necessary in these
stories and beliefs that have kept them alive across all of the
cultural changes between the oldest recorded tales and today.
Mythology and folklore abound with stories of these beings
and stories of humans who have been taken into their world or
wandered in unintentionally. Even in our thoroughly modern
western world the memory lingers and anecdotal accounts of
interactions with these beings still occur. Earth and Fairy, for
good or ill, seem intrinsically joined. But what is the Otherworld?

For the purposes of this book, we will be using the term fairy
(lower case f) in its most general sense to mean any and all of
the beings that come from or inhabit the world of Fairy (upper
case F). Some of these beings are human-looking some look like
animals and some look like nothing that we can easily describe.
Some are small and some are gigantic. Some are as powerful as
Gods – may indeed have been Gods – and some are much lower
on the scale of power. Our purpose here is to discuss the world
these beings inhabit but we will also in places be discussing the
beings as well because it is impossible to truly separate the two
topics entirely.

To understand these beings and the beliefs around them, I believe, we need to also understand their world and so this book is an attempt to gather together various culturally specific understandings of that world, including some modern pagan beliefs. There is a great deal more that could be said about the world of Fairy outside these specific cultures, particularly the closely related Norse Alfheims, but discussing that falls outside the scope of this book. It's also important to understand that while we will be using the terms Otherworld and Fairy interchangeably throughout for this concept there are culturally specific terms (mentioned in each chapter) and the terms Otherworld and Fairy were never universally used. I'm doing so here only for ease of discussion with what is a wider topic across these varied cultures.

Throughout western Europe, particularly in the Celtic, Anglo-Saxon, and related cultures, there has been a deeply rooted belief in and fascination with a place that is adjacent to the human world and perpetually connected to it. Across cultures this adjacent reality has gone by many names: the Otherworld, Fairy, Fairyland, An Saol Eile, Elfland, Avalon, Annwn. In every case and by any name this is a place of magic and enchantment, filled with beings who are alien to humanity yet inextricably connected to humans and the human world. It is a place of contradictions, of delights and dangers, which can entrap the unwary as easily as bless those who pass through it.

Understanding the world of Fairy is and will always be a challenge because there isn't any one cohesive view of it, nor is there any one longstanding understanding of it for people to study. It has always been a diverse place, shaped by a patchwork of stories and theories, stitched together into an often-contradictory narrative. This can make it a daunting task to try to study but diving deep into the various beliefs and stories is worthwhile as long as you can accept the inherent contradictions

which are as much a part of Fairy as the enchantment and magic that define it.

In our thoroughly modern world Fairy has been pushed to the fringes of fantasy and children's literature, moved from a place that any human might encounter to a place that is reached through imagination and story. The concept itself adapts across time and cultures but as newer meanings are added onto the older, we find that the original understandings also remain giving us a complex and nuanced place. And it is this complex and nuanced place, in all its layers, that we will strive to uncover here.

To begin, however, I think we must disambiguate some terms, which are widely used but whose meanings are too often vague or unclear, or in some cases different depending on the people we are speaking to. This understanding will be essential as we move forward into the undeniably muddy waters of Fairy, by any name.

Fae – also spelled fay[2] – is from the 12th century old French, likely from the older Latin Fata, meaning spirits of fate, and Williams suggests it entered French as a term for Celtic goddesses later shifting to women of supernatural power, then to an adjective meaning roughly enchanting, and finally to the place of Fairyland itself (Williams, 1991). This use for the place of Fairy is how the term enters English in the 13th century and we see it developing as both an adjective describing things with the nature of that place as well as a term for beings from that place. Briggs suggest that the initial adjective form may have been fay-erie, to indicate something that was enchanting or had an enchanting nature (Briggs, 1976). We find the term, as a noun, in Chaucer's *The Wife of Bath's Tale* as fayerye which was the middle English form. In early modern and modern English, the word shifted to fairy, under various spellings.

In the oldest English sources, we see fairy used as an adjective as well as a noun and this adjectival use continued for hundreds

8

of years. For example, in Milton's 17th century work *Paradise Lost*, book one line 781 he refers to *'fairy elves'* where fairy here is an adjective describing the elves. The noun is something of a catch all for any being from the land of Fairy or with a fairy-like nature and we see it used synonymously with elf, goblin, and incubi. This 16th century example from a poem by Alexander Montgomerie illustrates this well with fairy, elf, and incubi all being used interchangeably:

The King of Fairy, and his Court, with the Elf Queen, with many elvish Incubi was riding that night.

The terms don't have a fixed description or meaning beyond 'of Fairyland' and an implication of the enchanting and supernatural. Williams perhaps summarizes this variety of application best:

...fairy in particular, but more generally any supernatural name, is necessarily amorphous, and...from its earliest use in English... no single meaning has ever been paramount." (Williams, 1991).

Richard Firth Green in his 2016 book *Elf Queens and Holy Friars* says much the same, arguing that elf and fairy, which have been used interchangeably across the centuries, have never had a clear or fixed definition but have always been amorphous. This, naturally makes any discussion of the beings or the place more difficult.

The meaning of the terms remains vague through today with applications as an adjective and noun for both a place and beings from the place. We can find examples of fairy with both of these usages across folklore, modern anecdotes, and academia. Patricia Lysaght discusses the Bean Sidhe, an example where fairy is used as an adjective[3], in her book *The Banshee*. The Fairy Investigation Society's 2017 Fairy Census offers examples of fairy as applied to various described anecdotal accounts which cover a range of manifest forms. In some demographics the word fairy has become hyper-specialized to indicate only a type of small winged sprite, however, across many other demographics the word retains its older broader meanings. This dichotomy of use by different groups means that context may be required in order to understand what the word means within any source. An academic paper using the word fairy is likely to be adhering to the broader meaning, as are occurrences within folklore or traditional belief, but personal use or use within a specific group may follow the specialized meaning. This is an important distinction as the meanings have drifted so far from each other as to be nearly antithetical in nature now.

Fairy has multiple spellings across the written record because English had a non-standard orthography until relatively recently. This means that words were spelled in any way which might phonetically convey the sounds of the spoken word. Hence, we see fairy as everything from feirie to phary to faerye. There are 93 different variant spellings noted by Williams with fairy being the most common at 724 occurrences followed by faery at 131, fayry at 55, and faerie at 49 (Williams, 1991). In current academic and folklore usage fairy is the usual preferred spelling, however, as with the specialized meaning of fairy gaining popularity in some niches there has been an effort by some people to distinguish fairy from faery with the prior supposedly indicating twee, Victorian fairies and the latter supposedly indicating real or legitimate fairies. Similarly, there has also been a push in some demographics to use fae as a term to indicate Otherworldly beings generally where fairy is used to mean only a specific type. These spelling and semantic issues, as touched on in the previous paragraph, can cause confusion in communicating between people or groups ascribing different meanings to the terms. In this text we will be using the spelling 'fairy' primarily with the meaning defined broadly above, unless quoting a source which used an alternate spelling.

It should be noted that fairy and fae in modern usage are English language terms and have only existed as such for about 700 years. These do not reflect Christianization as Western Europe was Christian for several hundred years prior to fae coming into French (arguably with a strong pagan connotation initially) but rather the evolution of the languages, particularly English. There were and are non-English terms within the cultures that now use fairy in an English language context, and these terms pre-date the word fairy but often have related or parallel meanings in context. As previously touched on, the words elf and fairy are used interchangeably and that likely stems from the Anglo-Saxon term aelf which predates fairy but describes a similar type of being who was also equated later broadly to fairy, goblin, and incubus (Harper, 2020). In the same way in the Irish, we see the Daoine Sidhe or Aos Sidhe [people of the fairy hills] or sióga whose name intrinsically implies that connection to the sidhe, the fairy hills or Otherworld. The word sidhe – modern Irish sí – like the word fairy indicates both the place (fairy mounds) and, as an adjective, things with the nature of the place hence sidhe, fairy hills, but also slua sidhe, fairy host, or cú sidhe, fairy hound, and in modern slang sidhe can also be used to refer to the beings of that place. Every culture will have its own terms like this, for which the English fairy is simply the best equivalent term.

I'll point out that in many places there is a prohibition about using the term fairy and euphemisms are used instead. Euphemisms go back to at least the 14th century and can be found in across Celtic language speaking countries, as well as in older English material. One 16th century example from England uses the term Fair Folk in Latin, pulchrum populum (Green, 2016). The term Good Neighbours, in Scots, can be traced back to the 15th century. The concept behind the use of these terms rests in the belief that calling them fairies offended them and so one would want to use a term that was appealing or positive in case fairies passing by invisibly overheard the comment. This prohibition, however, does not seem to apply or have applied to the world of Fairy itself which doesn't have the same euphemistic terms around it.

This summarizes the pertinent information relating to these words, and hopefully may offer some clarity to the subject, which is admittedly opaque, as we go forward.

End Notes

1. A quick note about spelling. Until relatively recently English (like many languages) did not have standardized spelling which means that we can find a wide array of spellings for the word fairy in historic material. My preference is to use the spelling 'fairy' which is the most common across both academic material and Irish folklore.

2. Fae and fay not to be confused with fey, a Norse originating word for someone or something doomed or fated to die. Although there has been some speculation that fae/fay may relate to fey through the root concept of fate the terms themselves had different applications and seem to have been understood differently.

3. Lysaght's book is primarily focused on Irish language terms for the Bean Sidhe, however, she does touch on translations of these terms which reflect the use of fairy as an adjective.

Chapter 1

What Is the Otherworld?

It was not exactly dark, but a kind of twilight or gloaming. There were neither windows nor candles and he could not make out where the twilight came from, if not through the walls and roof. These were rough arches made of a transparent rock, incrusted with sheepsilver and rock spar, and other bright stones. But though it was rock, the air was quite warm, as it always is in Elfland.
– Childe Rowland

The Otherworld is known by many names: Fairy, An Saol Eile, Elfland, Fairyland, Annwn, Avalon. We will be discussing these more specifically in the following chapters, because each one has some important nuanced differences, however, to begin we need to establish the broad strokes that are similar across all of them. By any name the Otherworld may be generally understood as the same place, or at least sort of place, viewed through various cultural lenses, and therefore there are broad statements that we can make about it. The similarities found in the beliefs about this place in various cultures speaks to either a shared root belief or a shared experience and it is generally agreed by most scholars that there was at some point a universal Celtic[1], and possibly wider Indo-European, belief in the Otherworld often framed as Otherworldly islands. The roots of this belief then are very deep and find diverse expressions across a range of cultures, only some of which we'll be discussing in this book.

It is likely that the term 'Otherworld' itself, as well as the wider concept attached to the term, has come to us through a Christian lens and reflects the Christian separation of reality into this world and another world. The term is first found in Ireland used in Christian material and is likely sourced further from Lucan's writing on Druidic belief that suggested souls survived in another world after death, creating a dichotomy that was most likely not found in older pre-Christian belief as such (Sims-Williams, 2011). Rather than the very clearly delineated 'this world' and 'the other world' found in this belief it's likely that older views didn't see the worlds as so clearly or neatly separated, something that can still be found in folk belief where reaching the Otherworld may happen accidently or by passage through human world obstacles. While this doesn't mean we shouldn't use the term – it has been in use for a long time at this point – it does mean that we need to be careful not to fall into seeing a hard separation between the worlds as that isn't reflected in belief or in much of the existing material that we have. While we call it the Otherworld, it is a world that is layered on and intrinsically connected to the human one, in some stories directly interwoven with our reality. In some ways we might say that you can never truly separate our reality from the Otherworld or the Otherworld from our reality, and the two have a symbiotic existence. The Otherworld isn't the human world but it also isn't sharply divided from it, rather it is a small step sideways from the mundane reality we perceive.

Despite that fact, to begin it is best to understand the Otherworld *as* a world, as rich and diverse as the earth and perhaps as large and varied which is given continuity through the similarities shared across the wider beliefs but has unique expressions in every culture. Any narrow view of the Otherworld, of Fairy, will inevitably miss a great deal of nuance, and nuance is the key to everything that will follow. For every certainty there is a contradiction and for every answer there are three more questions; this is the nature of Fairy. As Patrick Sims-Williams more thoroughly explains in his book *Irish Influence on Medieval Welsh Literature* it is best to understand the Otherworld not as one vast place but as a variety of regional territories. In this way we can see that the Otherworld as it is perceived and understood in Ireland will be unique to what we find in Scotland or Wales or England; just as every human place is different from others while all are part of a wider whole so, too, we can understand the Otherworld the same way. Often the beliefs we find in each regional culture reflects the human culture of those places, so that, for example, Ireland has a variety of local fairy kingdoms which all exist as part of a wider Otherworld while England has a more cohesive single Otherworld with paired rulers. Understanding the specific cultures and time periods of the beliefs can be enormously helpful in understanding the wider beliefs around Fairy themselves.

There can be a tendency, since we are using one term for all of these places in general, to see them as more directly connected or related to each other than they actually are and we need to be careful about that. There are certainly many similarities in the beliefs about these various Otherworlds across these cultures but it is less likely – although possible – that this is because they all come from one traceable root concept and more likely that they reflect millennia of cultural exchange and interaction, wherein the belief in an Otherworld, shared by each group, influenced and shaped the understanding of that Otherworld in the other cultures. Or put another way the beliefs as we have them today are the result of a co-creative process; there is no strand of 'pure' belief to be found that isn't influenced and directed by other beliefs from other groups that culture has interacted with across time so that, for example, the Irish belief has been shaped by Welsh belief, Christian ideas, and within the last few centuries by popular cultural ideas from England and the US. We are looking at a tapestry of material woven together, tightly, over time not separate branches growing from one tree.

The true nature and location of the Otherworld is and will always be unknown, although there are many ideas about it. Some people firmly believe that the Otherworld is a place adjacent to and connected to – but separate from – the human world.

For others it is a world that exists overlapped onto the human world and only ever a perceptual shift away. For some the Otherworld is a different dimension from the human world but one that is tethered to it, sometimes referred to as extradimensional or interdimensional. These views are each true and can be found in descriptions from folklore and mythology as well as anecdotal accounts but they are each only a piece of the truth, and perhaps a piece influenced by the individual perceiving them. Ultimately the true nature and location of the Otherworld remains as mysterious as it had always been, something that we may be able to begin to understand in hints and glimpses but that we may never fully comprehend. What we can do here, however, is discuss some of the main characteristics that apply to different iterations of this world across cultures and which help us begin to paint the picture of what this world is.

The Otherworld as a chthonic world is one of its most cohesive features; it is a place under the ground or associated with being beneath the earth. This is, of course, not exactly a literal view although it isn't entirely figurative either. The belief seems to have been that the Otherworld was both literally in the ground and also that the earth was merely a passageway into the realm itself. There is no cohesion here with the views and we must understand that this cannot be reconciled in any simple way. So, we have stories of people digging into the ground to get into one of the fairy mounds, for example, and also stories of people who step into a passageway only to find themselves in a vast realm that is clearly too large to be contained in a hill or mound. This reflects the idea discussed above of the Otherworld as both adjoining the human world and joined to it.

It is sometimes understood as an Underworld but that is at best an oversimplification. It contains beings that we may, depending on our personal lens, classify as underworld-like but it is not an underworld in the wider understanding of such a place as the realm of the human dead. Although it is true that some human dead do end up in the world of Fairy it is not the ultimate destination of all humans who die and conflating the two causes a great deal of confusion. It would be better to understand the Underworld, as such, as a separate place that is further from human life and the Otherworld as a place closer and more intrinsically tied to human life.

The Otherworld is a place that is part of and also apart from the human world. It is not a heaven in any sense and is much more direct and relatable to human life than any concept of heaven would be, full of fighting, feasting, and sex[2]. It is a place that is here and also not-here and which a person may wander into unwittingly or search for across a lifetime and never find.

As we dig further into this, it's important to remember that, as is hinted at above, there is no one cohesive understanding of the Otherworld and what it is, just as the world itself isn't one single place. What we have instead is a variety of theories about what the Otherworld is each shaped by the individual's personal lens as well as cultural lens. None of these are right or wrong and all should be considered.

Overlapping Reality with Our Own

By this understanding the realm of the Otherworld is directly layered onto the human realm but most humans lack the ability to perceive it. The fairies are, in this view, truly our neighbours living side by side with us but imperceptible to the normal human senses. Even within this understanding, however, the Otherworld is seen as more than simply an invisible layer to the human world and may contain a greater depth than the corresponding human location. This view may be reflected in older beliefs which conflated real world places, including the Isle of Man and Ireland, with Otherworldly islands where both realities – Otherworldly island and human world place – existed simultaneously in belief.

Connected but Different Reality

In this view the Otherworld is a reality which is adjoining the human one but which is not identical to it and may follow different rules. The most striking difference is usually a notable increase in magic and a different flow of time. There have also been stories of humans encountering a world of Fairy where basic laws of reality seem altered or sharply different, such as accounts in the ballad material of a world without sun or moon. In modern terms this view sometimes refers to the Otherworld as interdimensional or extradimensional.

Chthonic Realm

A common understanding of the Otherworld in academia describes it as a chthonic realm, or in simpler terms a world that is in or under the earth. How literally this view is taken varies widely with some seeing it as largely metaphoric and others seeing it more literally. The mythology and folklore can support both views, with stories that imply digging into a fairy mound will reach those living within it, and others making it clear that a hill acts as a gateway or door to an adjoining place.

Energetic Realm

A more modern, but sometimes popular, idea describes the Otherworld as a purely energetic rather than tangible place. In this view the Otherworld may be comparable to or the same as the astral realm and is not physical at all. This particular view is probably the most controversial because it does directly contradict older folklore and folk belief but it is found throughout belief systems influenced by theosophy and the new age movement. This view also tends to favour the idea that humans have a great deal of power or influence over the Otherworld.

Separate Dimension

Another view of the Otherworld is that it is an entirely separate dimension or reality that can be reached or travelled to but which isn't inherently connected to or overlapping the human world.

Perhaps the defining characteristic of the Otherworld, beyond every other thing we've discussed so far, is that it is the home to beings we call fairies in English, who in turn are defined by the fact they come from this world. It is the embodiment of a logical fallacy and yet also true, a mobius strip of cause and effect, which in many ways illustrates the contradictions inherent in everything related to fairies. They are what they are because they come from the world of Fairy, and yet that world is what it is because it is their home.

This leads us into the question of what fairies are, but that isn't easily answered. It is sometimes easier to say what fairies aren't than to clarify what they are, but what we can say for certain, based on the long-term understandings of what fairies are across western Europe, is that they are beings of the Otherworld, literally 'of Fairy'. Are some of them what we might now call nature spirits? Are some of them human dead? Are some pagan Gods? Yes, some fall into each of those groups. But no one category or explanation fits all of them. These are beings who are from the Otherworld yet can and do interact with humans and can pass between their world and ours at their discretion.

The best way to understand what fairies are is to appreciate the nuances. There is no simple answer. Rather, what we see is a diverse grouping that encompasses an array of Otherworldly spirits and land spirits which we label fairies for convenience. Hundreds, if not thousands, of different kinds of named and even unnamed types of beings fall into this wide category and it makes sense that there is no easy way to understand them all as a whole beyond the broadest strokes.

Having now established all the contradictions that define the Otherworld, and to some degree the beings within it, there are some basic features that are found across various cultural depictions. These form a rough guideline to what is and isn't the Otherworld across sources:

No Sun or Moon

In many descriptions of the Otherworld, it is clearly stated that while there is ambient lighting, sometimes described as a perpetual twilight, there are no visible sun or moon in the sky. In some sources, like the 'Ballad of Thomas the Rhymer', the Otherworld is described as existing without stars as well.

Different Reality

In many ways the Otherworld is similar to the human world: there are trees and grass and rivers and the same kinds of geography we can find around us, although sometimes the geography described by those who've journeyed there isn't like the real-world geography of the place the human lives. But that said there are notable differences as well including animals and sometimes plants that can speak, operant magic, shapeshifting, and occasionally things that defy human-world physics.

Time

Consistent across the varied cultural beliefs is the idea that time flows differently on earth and in the world of Fairy. A day here might be a year or years in the Otherworld, and in the same way a night in Fairy might be a decade or centuries. In the story of Niamh and Oisín the three years Oisín spends in the Otherworld equal 300 years in Ireland while in an anecdotal account from England a man who claimed to spend several years in Fairy was only missing from earth for a matter of minutes.

Animals

This may go without saying but to be clear, the Otherworld is not only full of beings who are roughly humanoid in appearance as well as shapeshifters, but also with an array of animals that are in most ways like their earthly counterparts, although usually described as superior to them. For example, Lady Wilde in her book *Ancient Legends, Mystic Charms, and Legends of Ireland* describes the horses of the Aos Sidhe [people of the fairy hills] this way:

> ...the breed of horses they reared could not be surpassed in the world–fleet as the wind, with the arched neck and the broad chest and the quivering nostril, and the large eye that showed they were made of fire and flame, and not of dull, heavy earth. (Wilde, 1888)

Reversal of Seasons

A common motif found across a range of beliefs, including Irish and English, is that the season in Fairy will be at odds with the season in the human world. In the Echtra Nera, for example, Nera goes to stay in the Otherworld but must leave to warn his human friends about a pending attack from the fairy host; he fears he won't be believed and his fairy wife tells him to take some fresh spring plants with him as it is late autumn/early winter at his home. Rev Robert Kirk's account of the Scottish fairies claims that when humans have abundant food the fairies experience lean times, also possibly referencing a reversal of seasons wherein the fairies would be in late winter or early spring when humans were harvesting crops[3].

Abundance

Although modern views have moved away from this, older folkloric and literature accounts of the Otherworld emphasize its richness. It is ubiquitously a place of treasure and of sustenance, although both often present a threat to humans who venture there, either through temptation or a magical ability to trap the unwary. Castles and keeps in Fairy are often said to be built or heavily decorated with gold and fine jewels, and things like good food and drink are abundant.

Separation from Human Life or the Human World

A key feature across belief about the Otherworld is that it is not synonymous with the human world or human life. It is a place that might mirror many aspects of human life but also often reverses or inverts human mores and expectations. It exists separated from human reality in both the figurative and literal senses, being a different type of reality and also existing away from mortal perceptions. In modern terms we might say it is divided from the human world by a veil, 'the veil between worlds', although that concept is newer. In older contexts the separation was sometimes described as a magic mist which kept the realities distinct and other times as a spell which hid Fairy from human eyes. In all cultural accounts it is a place that cannot be perceived or reached via normal means.

The other main defining characteristic of the Otherworld across all its iterations is its liminality. This is fully explored in Piotr Spyra's 2015 article 'The Terrors of the Threshold' as he dissects fairy themes in Sir Orfeo but to summarize here, liminality is a concept of being between two things, wherein something is both and neither what it is between. Dawn and twilight, for example, are liminal times which exist between night and day. The shore is a liminal place which is between ocean and land. These are times and places which exist straddling two opposing things – day and night, sand and sea – but are themselves neither wholly one or the other. That is liminality. The people of Fairy are a liminal people neither living nor dead, neither mortal or immortal, neither in the human world nor separate from it. The world of Fairy is a liminal place which exists anchored in the human world by fairy hills and fairy trees but is not wholly in this world. Or as Spyra puts it:

> *In these traditions, the land of fairies is never the far-off country of literary fairy tales that requires a seven-league-boots journey across distant mountains; quite the opposite, it is right there, right next to the most familiar, or even mundane spaces of everyday life, and may perhaps best be visualized as a sort of a parallel universe, to which places such as fairy mounds or local hilltops provide immediate access.* (Spyra, 2015).

This idea of liminality is echoed by Rev. Robert Kirk in *The Secret Commonwealth of Elves, Fauns, and Fairies* where he describes the fairy folk as being neither solid nor intangible but having bodies which existed in a fluid state between the two and could become fully either. When we explore stories of Fairy in any context liminality is a hallmark of the world.

Beyond this there will be cultural or regionally specific beliefs that shape the Otherworld in slightly different directions and give each view a uniqueness. We will be tackling each of these variations in the following chapters to explore the world of Fairy as fully as possible.

End Notes

1. Celtic in this context is used to refer to a group of cultures which shared languages and root languages. I may also refer to them as Celtic language speaking cultures. There is an ongoing debate about the use of the term in academia as it can be imprecise and may be seen as outdated.

2. I'd go with the alliteration here but I don't want to offend anyone. I'm sure readers can guess the logical word to place here.

3 The harvest season would generally begin at some point in July and run through October; if this reversal of seasons is true then we would expect the fairies to be in what would be equivalent to January/February when the human harvest begins in July/August.

Chapter 2

An Saol Eile

I saw a radiant, free land.
where falsehoods or deceptions are not spoken
Laeg describing Mag Mell in the Serglige Con Chulainn

An Saol Eile is the Irish name for the Otherworld or what elsewhere is called Fairy. It seems to be a more modern term as opposed to Domun Aile, the older Irish used in myths like the Táin Bó Fraích. Since Saol Eile is more popularly used than the older domhan eile that's what we will use here. I will note though that saol means both world and life, while domhan means world or earth, so there is a fine semantic difference between the two concepts. Although the name is different, and the specific mythology, the general concept is the same and the two are usually viewed synonymously. In Ireland we also find specific locations mentioned including: Mag Mell [Pleasant Plain], Tír Tairngire [Land of Promise], Tír fo Thuinn [Land under the Waves], Emhain Abhlach [Emhain of the Apples], and the well-known Tír na nÓg [Land of the Young]. These all represent specific locations within the wider realm of the Otherworld although they are sometimes used synonymously with the Otherworld itself. To further muddy the waters the term sidhe [old/middle Irish side] is also used synonymously as a term for the Otherworld although it more literally means 'fairy hills'; this has caused some people to falsely conflate the fairy hills and Otherworld to a degree that they believe only the hills represent this place or the entryway to it. In Irish folk belief, however, this is untrue and we see a wide array of locations associated with the Otherworld including islands, hills, underground, and under water in the ocean or in lakes

(Gray, 1983; Houlihan, 2022). Lone Hawthorn trees were also associated with the Good Folk and thought to be their homes, or gateways to their homes. Strong prohibitions existed and continue to exist that people should never damage a place or tree belonging to the aos sidhe, because they will take their revenge at any harm done to what belongs to them.

The most common term for the places that anchor the Otherworld in the human world is sidhe, modern Irish sí, meaning fairy hill or Otherworldly mound and this is where we get the term aos sidhe, people of the fairy hills. Other terms often associate with these places are ráth or lios for the old forts or dún for the old strongholds; these are often bronze or iron age archaeological sites which have been reclaimed by the earth, appearing now as hills, although some of them include the remains of earthworks or stone buildings. One of the most well-known of these locations may be Sid in Broga [Newgrange] which is the home of the Tuatha De Danann God Angus mac ind Óc and is a famous neolithic monument. There has been much speculation across the years that belief in the aos sidhe and the importance of the sidhe are rooted in their being ancient burial locations, connecting the aos sidhe directly to the human ancestors, however, it should be kept in mind that not all of the sidhe or various locations related to the aos sidhe are burial sites or connected to the human dead. The picture is too complex to be given any single explanation.

Whether the Otherworld exists literally within these physical locations or not is uncertain. In early accounts the sidhe are described as beneath the earth or across the water but are described as physical places themselves, sometimes even conflated with actual geographic places like the Isle of Man or Arran Islands. In later mythology and folk belief, the idea of the sidhe as the home of the Gentry continued but the hills themselves were seen as existing in Ireland and acting as doorways or gateways between the worlds. There are 18th and 19th century anecdotal accounts of people who saw doors in these hills opened up, revealing great halls, and accounts in folklore of people who entered into the Otherworld through these hills and found themselves in another world entirely. In Echtra Nera the sidhe of Cruachan is entered through a cave but is itself an entire landscape complete with a fort and homes. However, we do have stories as well of humans who dug into a fairy mound in order to force the inhabitants out or as acts of war, such as the angry husband whose wife was taken by Finnbheara who dug into Knockma and salted the earth to gain her return. There are also a handful of stories in myth or folklore, such as Echtra Chormaic i Tír Tairngiri, where a person wanders into a mist and finds themselves in the Otherworld when they emerge on the other side. In *Altram Tige Da Medar* an Saol Eile is a place that exists side by side with the human world but which is invisible to humans, except only on Samhain [around 31 October] when the magic hiding them isn't active. Thus, the Irish Otherworld exists within the sidhe or fairy mounds but is also a series of Otherworldly islands, usually said to be reached by sailing west and sometimes said to be visible looking west from the Irish coast and in places it is also found beneath lakes, such as at Loch Gur, or reached through caves such as the sidhe of Cruachan. All of these views exist simultaneously and without contradiction, placing an Saol Eile as a truly liminal concept which is both within the earth and distinct from it, both on land and at sea, both part of the human world and apart from it.

The oldest written account of Fairy comes to us from the Irish, in the 9th century[1] Echtra Condla [Adventures of Connla] where a woman of Fairy comes to Ireland and woos Connla the son of the king. Connla agrees to leave with her and go live among her people in the sidhe, or the fairy hills, and to do this the two go to the shore and travel away on a boat. This is particularly interesting to note because although the term 'fairy hills' is used in several places the means of getting there is a journey over water, which ties into wider ideas in early Irish literature that the Otherworld is an island or islands which must be reached by extraordinary means.

Let us now look at some of these named islands in more depth:

Tír na nÓg – Land of Youth or Land of the Young, possibly the most well-known of the Otherworldly islands. Most famously known from the story of Niamh and Oisín, wherein the sidhe woman Niamh came to Ireland and convinced Fionn Mac Cumhaill's son Oisín to return with her to Tír n nÓg. McKillop suggests that this island is sometimes said to be located in Liscannor Bay, co Clare, citing an 1861 source which claimed Tír na nÓg was seen as a shining city amidst the waves there.

Mag Mell – one of the names of the Otherworldly land ruled by the god Manannán mac Lir, who is also sometimes said to be the King of the Otherworld more generally, Mag Mell means 'pleasant plain'. It is often referred to as an island although in at least one account it is called a fort.

Tír Tairngiri – literally 'land of promise' this term is used for the Irish Otherworld and Christian Heaven or the 'promised land' of the Old Testament. Although not ruled directly by Manannán mac Lir it is often associated with him and also is often the goal of various Echtra stories (McKillop, 1998).

Emhain Abhlach – place of apples, the Otherworldly island home and kingdom of Manannán mac Lir. One of the main Otherworldly islands we will discuss Emhain Abhlach in detail below.

Tír fo Thuinn – also sometimes called Tír na Thonn, Land under Waves or Land of Waves. An Otherworldly realm that exists beneath the sea and appears in a story of the Fianna.

Tír na mBan – land of women. An Otherworldly island encountered in several Imram stories of Irish myth. Tír na mBan is a place filled with beautiful women and the best foods, where the women willingly pair up with men who travel there and offer them fine hospitality (McKillop, 1998). As with any other island of the Otherworld it cannot be reached through normal means but only through extraordinary ones or accidentally and is notable for the way that time works differently there so that a year there will be decades or centuries in the human world.

Tír na mBéo – 'the land of the living' although less literally it could be read as the land of eternal or perpetual life. Described as a land of peace and plenty.

Hy Breasail – the name is of an unknown meaning but folk etymology has long claimed it comes from Uí Breasail meaning descendants of Bresail; in contrast McKillop suggests the source as í – island, and bres – beauty, hence beautiful island (McKillop, 1998). Hy Breasail is a mysterious island said to exist to the far west of Ireland which is a place of perfect happiness without work or contention. It can be seen on many maps in the medieval period, sometimes under the name Brasil, and was said in folk belief to be the home of the Tuatha De Danann as well as other mythic Irish heroes (MacKillop, 1998).

The Nature of An Saol Eile

In the Echtra Condla the fairy woman who comes to woo Connla to go with her to the Otherworld describes her home this way:

"an immortal land where there is no death or the sin of transgressions. We have our harvest feast without labour; peace cloaks us without strife." (Daimler, 2022).

In the Ulster cycle, which is quoted at the start of this chapter, we see Mag Mell being described as a place where no one lies and which is *'radiant and free'*. These ideas are further reiterated by Kim McCone in his *Pagan Past and Christian Present in Early Irish Literature* where he discusses the Otherworld as a paradise free of sin and free of lying. The Otherworld is a place where there is no sickness, death, sin, or suffering and which is full of goodness and abundance. However, there is violent death to be found there and while several sources do describe it as 'without strife' we have many stories of battles which occur there. In the Echtra Laegaire meic Crimthain, for example, we find a man of the sidhe approaching human warriors for aid in a battle in the sidhe, where the humans go into the Otherworld to aid him by travelling beneath a lake. Once there they engage in what is described as a slaughterous battle against the sidhe-man's enemies until they defeat them and the fort of Mag Mell is taken. *Altram Tige Da Medar* describes Angus flying into a rage in his Otherworldly home of Sid in Broga and attacking his brother Finnbheara and Finnbheara's people, driving them out. So, while we might describe an Saol Eile as an idyllic place, it is not exempt from the dangers of the human world. In the same way it is distinct from the Christian ideas of heaven as – with rare exceptions – it includes all the hedonism a person might dream of from abundant feasting to lovers to fine clothing and jewels.

A section from the Imramm Brain, or Voyage of Bran, does the best job of describing what the Irish Otherworld – and Emhain Abhlach in particular – are like. As with the descriptions we've already discussed here we find Emhain Abhlach as a place of wonders and beauty, without sickness or death. It is an island out in the sea, surrounded by waves and held up by four pillars of white bronze, and described as *'A delight of the eyes, a glorious range'*. It is full of flowering trees and birds which sing at every hour, a place where *'every colour glistens'* and which contains *'nothing rough or harsh'*, a place without weeping or betrayal, filled with joy and beautiful music.

'Without grief, without sorrow, without death,
Without any sickness, without debility,
That is the sign of Emhain--
Uncommon is an equal marvel.
'A beauty of a wondrous land,
Whose aspects are lovely,
Whose view is a fair country,
Incomparable is its haze. (Nutt, 1895)

The narrator describes it as place full of jewels and treasure, with chariots of gold, silver, and bronze. Along with this Emhain Abhlach has the best of foods and wine, flowing with honey, and its horses are described as:

Yellow golden steeds are on the sward there,
Other steeds with crimson hue,
Others with wool upon their backs
Of the hue of heaven all-blue. (Nutt, 1895)

The music and laughter of Emhain Abhlach is full of joy at all times, and its inhabitants are the most beautiful and skilled, clad in gold and silver and cloth of every colour. The people entertain themselves with music, singing, and games of sport like racing as well as games of skill (presumably Fidchell, a game somewhat like chess).

A particular feature of Emhain Abhlach that we are told of is that for its inhabitants the ocean is like dry land, and the animals of the sea are like its livestock:

'The sheen of the main, on which thou art,
The white hue of the sea, on which thou rowest about,
Yellow and azure are spread out,
It is land, and is not rough.

38. 'Speckled salmon leap from the womb
Of the white sea, on which thou lookest:
They are calves, they are coloured lambs
With friendliness, without mutual slaughter.
39. 'Though (but) one chariot-rider is seen
In Mag Mell of many flowers,
There are many steeds on its surface,
Though them thou seest not. (Nutt, 1895)

There is much emphasis placed on the idea of Emhain Abhlach as a perfect place, abundant in all good things but exempt from death, age, and sin:

43. 'A wood with blossom and fruit,
On which is the vine's veritable fragrance,
A wood without decay, without defect,
On which are leaves of golden hue.
44. 'We are from the beginning of creation
Without old age, without consummation of earth,
Hence we expect not that there should be frailty,
The sin has not come to us (Nutt, 1895)

Beings of the Otherworld

The inhabitants who are found in an Saol Eile are equally complex, including the Tuatha De Danann, the aos sidhe, human dead, and various other fantastic beings like the Fir Bolg and Fomorians. The primary named figures of the Irish Otherworld are the Tuatha De Danann, who are often conflated with the aos sidhe but also exist in mythology as a group outside the aos sidhe. As Mark Williams says in his book *Ireland's Immortals*:

The Tuatha De Danann are presented throughout [the Acallam na Senorach] as completely synonymous with the people of the síd. They inhabit a series of apparently separate parallel worlds, a hidden archipelago stippling the landscape of Ireland as islands stud a sea. It is also worth bearing in mind that the Tuatha De Danann in the Acallam are legion – a people, not a pantheon... (Williams, 2016).

Various accounts imply that the Otherworld was inhabited before the Tuatha De Danann entered into it, including the *Altram Tige Da Medar* which tells us that Manannán as King of the Otherworld distributed the various sidhe to the Tuatha De Danann when they first came to live there. In the Cath Maige Tuired the Fomorians warriors are referred to as the Riders of the sidhe, and in later folklore we find many beings associated with the Otherworld or aos sidhe who are clearly not of the Tuatha De Danann. In myth and folklore, we also see the idea that some humans can be taken into the fairy throng, either stolen while they are still alive or appearing among the aos sidhe after death. In older sources only living humans who are taken are incorporated into the sidhe and many descriptions, as noted above, refer to an Saol Eile as a land without death or knowledge of death; in later folklore this was expanded to include those who died or at least appear to have died. Evans-Wentz's *Fairy Faith in Celtic Countries* recounts several anecdotal accounts from Ireland of people who saw people among the Good Folk who the human community believed had died. The School's Collection at Duchas.ie mentions the same as well as including accounts of changelings, that is fairies or enchanted objects left behind in the guise of stolen humans; the changeling would usually sicken and die to be buried by the human family while the stolen human lived on among the aos sidhe.

Discussing the rulers of the Irish Otherworld is somewhat more complex than in other contexts. Generally speaking, the Irish sidhe are monarchies, but various areas held by named personages are their own kingdoms rather than one wider unified group; within a specific territory there would be one or more known hills or locations, usually of a more impressive nature, associated with the ruler and many other smaller sidhe that fell under their rule (Houlihan, 2022). That said the situation is more complicated than we might imagine, with the various kingdoms belonging to the larger grouping of the aos sidhe and sometimes coming together for a unified purpose while at other times the various groups engage in warfare or competition with each other. They are therefore neither truly distinct nor truly united, but exist in a liminal place that includes both concepts.

The issue is also complicated because, while folklore gives us a variety of named kings and queens of the sidhe, technically each of the leading members of the Tuatha De Danann could be considered such. When the Tuatha De were driven into the sidhe by the Milesians, the leaders among them each claimed a specific sidhe for themselves and acted then as the ruler of that specific place. However, only certain figures became known as kings or queens of the sidhe in folklore. For our purposes here we will be looking at the ones known in folklore rather than exploring every named Tuatha De associated with a specific sidhe[2]. For those interested in a deeper dive into the names and specific locations associated with them I recommend they look to Chapter 4 of Michal Houlihan's book *Irish Fairies*.

Kings of the Otherworld

Manannán – the most often spoken of in mythology as a King of the Otherworldly is probably Manannán mac Lir, a somewhat mysterious figure who appears in Irish, Welsh, and Manx mythology[3]. According to the *Altram Tige Da Medar*, it was Manannán who assigned the Tuatha De Danann to the various fairy hills when they went into the Otherworld and who taught them to live in that world.

Dáire – an obscure figure who appears as the King of Tír Tairngire in the Echtra Airt meic Cuinn. He is said to be without any transgression and lived in chaste happiness with his wife, only coming together once to conceive their son (McKillop, 1998).

Kings of the Sidhe

Dagda – in the story 'In De Gabail an t-Sida' we are told that the Dagda was the one who the assigned each of the Tuatha De Danann new homes within the fairy mounds and the Dagda is said in the Aislinge Oengusso to be the King of all the sidhe in Ireland.

Finnbheara – in some later folklore the title of King of all the sidhe was given to the Dagda's youngest son, Finnbheara, who was also the King of the sidhe of Galway. His particular home is at Knockma and there is abundant folklore about him there, where he is known to entertain mortals and steal human women.

Bodb Dearg – Bodb the Red or Red Bodb, a son of the Dagda who was also a King of the sidhe of Munster. His main residency is said to be at Sidhe ar Femen on Sleivenamon. Bodb is an important figure across myth and folklore, serving as King of the Tuatha De Danann at one point and showing up in the Ulster cycle tale of the Quarrel of the Two Pig Keepers as well as the Aislinge Oengusso where he helps the Dagda and Oengus find the identity of the woman who has been plaguing Oengus's dreams.

Donn – also called Donn Fírinne, a King of the sidhe and the first of the Gaels or Milesians to die in Ireland, hance the first ancestor. Donn's special place is Oileann Buí or Bull rock off the coast of Co Cork; according to myth all who die must go there before passing on. He is also associated with Cnoc Fírinne in Munster near Rathkeale. He is said to appear sometimes as a horseman on a white horse and storms are associated with him (Ó hÓgáin, 2006).

Ochaill Oichni – named as the King of the sidhe of Connacht in the De Chophur in Da Muccida.

Midhir – king at Brí Leith or Sidhe Midir in Ardagh and a member of the Tuatha De Danann he is most well-known from the Tochmarc Etaine, which tells the story of how he lost and regained his wife Etain.

Queens of the Sidhe

Una – the wife of Finnbheara, Una is a Queen of the sidhe in her own right with a fairy hill of her own at Knocksheegowna. In one folktale Una was known to drive off anyone who dared go on her hill until one particular shepherd faced her down; despite the horrific forms she presented to him, he wasn't afraid and when she took the form of a great cow he jumped on her back and held on as she leapt from hilltop to hilltop. She so admired his courage that she allowed him to graze his sheep on her hill afterwards.

Clíodhna – a fairy queen in Cork Clíodhna is also sometimes said to be Queen of the mná sidhe [banshees]. She is one of the Tuatha De Danann, the daughter of Gebann, the druid of Manannán mac Lir and her sister is the fairy queen Aoibheall. In folklore she associated with the shore at Glendore, Cork, and a place called Carraig Chlíona [Cliodhna's rock] at Kilshannig (Ó hÓgáin, 2006; Houlihan, 2022).

Áine – Associated with both the hill of Cnoc Áine and Loch Gur in co Limerick, Áine is named as one of the Tuatha De Danann and also in folk belief as a fairy queen. Processions to her were made at Cnoc Áine at midsummer and she was sometimes seen sitting and combing her hair next to the lake.

Aoibheall – Queen of the sidhe of Crag Liath and the surrounding area near Killaloe, Aoibheall was associated with the older human kingdom of Thurmond as well as the Dal Cais and descendants of Brian Boru; it's said that she took one of Brian's sons as her lover and appeared to Brian before the battle of Clontarf to warn him of his impending death.

Aoife – featuring in mythology as a wife of Lir in the Fate of the Children of Lir and as a woman of the sidhe who is cursed into the form of a crane in the tale of Manannán's crane bag, Aoife is referred to as a fairy queen "of the north", by implication, in an 1854 exorcism against a Leannán sidhe (Transactions of the Ossianic Society, 1854).

End Notes

1. The text has been dated to the 9th century, however, the language used in it has been dated further back to at least the 7th century. Beveridge in her book Children into Swans suggests a possible date as early as the 5th century.
2. For example, the Morrigan is associated with the sidhe of Cruachan also known as Uaimh na gCait, which is referred to as her 'fit abode' in the Dindshenchas of Odras, however, the Morrigan is not widely known as a fairy queen in Irish folklore so is not being included as one here.
3. In Welsh and Manx myth he has a slightly different name; in all versions his name roughly translates to 'Manx one'.

Chapter 3

Elfland

And see not ye that bonny road,
That winds about the fernie brae?
That is the road to fair Elfland,
Where thou and I this night maun gae
Ballad of Thomas the Rhymer

In Scotland the common terms for the Otherworld were Elfland[1], Elphyne, Elfhame or Elfame [literally elf home], as elf and fairy were used synonymously until very recently, as well as Fairyland. Generally, Elfland is described as very similar to Fairy as we find it in the bulk of material elsewhere, that is it is a place that is simultaneously overlayed on mortal earth and distinct from it. The Elfland of Scotland existed on and beneath the earth, within the fairy hills and on islands whose locations moved or could only be accessed at certain times, rather than in an airy realm (McNeill, 1956). In many accounts the Fair Folk, or elves, would appear from these places to steal away mortals back to the Otherworld, while humans might rarely see glimpses of these places but couldn't access them without Otherworldly guidance (McNeill, 1956). It was a place that was a part of the human world but also separated from it, or at least from human perception of it, although some few humans gifted with special vision could see it without fairy aid.

The island Otherworld of Scotland is, again as with the Irish, said to be in the west; McNeil asserts that the archipelago of St Kilda, the western most islands of the Outer Hebrides, were often conflated with these mystical Otherworldly islands, for example, as she suggests the Arran islands were in Ireland.

This conflation of earthly islands with Otherworldly ones isn't unknown or uncommon and presents no conflict in a belief system that sees these places as existing in both worlds by nature anyway. In the same way we see the Gaidhlig word sìth[2] means both a physical hill as well as a fairy hill, and in Scots the word knowe, indicates a hillock and also often a fairy place. This isn't because every hill is a fairy hill but because there's an understanding of an overlapping association. In various accounts entrances to Elfland can be found near lone thorn trees, in or on hills, in glens, in meadows, and near certain wells; Several Scottish witchcraft trial accounts link the fairies and Fairyland to lakes as well (Henderson & Cowan, 2007). All of these places may perhaps be understood as liminal spaces and all represent connection points between Elfland and the human world which act as entrances or gateways from the human world to the other.

Descriptions of Elfland can be found across folklore but are perhaps most poetically relayed in the ballad material. It is here, particularly in the ballads of 'Tam Lin' and of 'Thomas the Rhymer', that we find some of the most evocative depictions of Elfland – interchangeably called Fairyland – which are echoed in other descriptions. As with the Irish an Saol Eile we find that Elfland is envisioned as a place without illness or suffering and one in which the rules of human physics are far more fluid:

> *But we that live in Fairy-land*
> *No sickness know nor pain*
> *I quit my body when I will,*
> *And take to it again.*
> *'I quit my body when I please,*
> *Or unto it repair;*
> *We can inhabit at our ease*
> *In either earth or air.*

'Our shapes and size we can convert
To either large or small;
An old nut-shell's the same to us
As is the lofty hall.
We sleep in rose-buds soft and sweet
We revel in the stream;
We wanton lightly on the wind
Or glide on a sunbeam.
"And all our wants are well supplied
From every rich man's store,
Who thankless sins the gifts he gets,
And vainly grasps for more.'
"And pleasant are our fairie sports,
We flie o'er hill and dale
But at the end of seven years
They pay the teen [tithe] to hell
The ballad of Tam Lin (Scott, 1802)

Tam Lin describes Elfland as a pleasant place and is clear that he would be happy to live in it forever if it weren't for the tithe to Hell which he fears he'll be used to pay. This passage also echoes wider ideas that fairies have the ability to be either physical or intangible at will, can change their sizes, and steal supplies from humans who speak ill of their own things or are too greedy. We get another version of Elfland with some differing details in the 'Wee Wee Man':

"It's down beneath yon bonny green bower
Though you must come with me and see."
We roved on and we sped on
Until we came to a bonny green ha'
The room was made of the beaten gold

And pure as crystal was the gla'.
There were pipers playing on every spare
And ladies dancing in glistering green
He clapped his hands, down came the mist
And the man in the ha' no more was seen. (Scott, 1802)

In contrast to Tam Lin's more pastoral description here we find Elfland with a room made of gold and fine, clear glass windows 'pure as crystal', and green-clad women dancing to the music of pipers. Green being often understood as the fairies' special colour we see it referenced three times across the ten lines, used for the fine leafy area under which or through which Elfland is reached as well as the hall within it and the clothing of the women.

'The ballad of Thomas the Rhymer' describes the journey to Elfland in great detail but offers very little on what the place itself is like, beyond claiming that all the blood shed on earth flows in the streams and rivers of Fairy. The older prose version, 'Thomas of Erceldoune', offers slightly more detail in the passage where he recounts being brought to the Fairy Queen's castle, which he says is full of fine ladies and knights, much joy and revelry, music and entertainment, and a great feast of fifty roasted stags (Murray, 1875). In other words, it is a place full of everything a person might want to enjoy and be surrounded by.

Another exceptional source for information on the Scottish beliefs around fairies and Elfland can be found in the writings of reverend Robert Kirk who discusses the Good Folk of Scotland at length, including the nature of their dwellings. This is a particularly important source because it is one of the most detailed early modern accounts. As Kirk would have it the realm of the Good Folk is quite literally subterranean – a term he also uses for the beings themselves – although as he describes the Fair Folk as having bodies that are *'like a condensed cloud'* and only of a partially physical nature one might suppose their world is also not purely physical. Kirk goes on to describe the houses of these beings in this realm thusly:

> *Their Houses are called large and fair, and (unless at some odd occasions) unperceivable by vulgar eyes, like Rachland, and other enchanted Islands, having fire Lights, continual Lamps, and Fires, often seen without Fuel to sustain them.* (Kirk & Lang, 1893)

According to Kirk the food that is found in this subterranean Elfland is stolen from mortal earth, brought there by some unknown means, and the people of the hills delight in mimicking human culture including both dress and ceremonies. Despite this Kirk does also claim the Good Folk have their own language which he describes as speaking *"by way of whistling, clear, not rough"* as well as their own *'doings'* including meetings, fights, injuries, and funerals as he has it *"both in the Earth and Air"* (Kirk & Lang, 1893).

The above descriptions are all echoed or elaborated on in accounts given by accused witches and cunningfolk, who talk of an Elfland that is fine and beautiful. Alison Pearson said that Fairyland was full of good music and high spirits; Isobel Gowdie talked of a place that was both beautiful and bountiful; Donald McIlmichall described a great hall lit with numerous candles, at a time when candles were a rare luxury (Henderson & Cowan, 2007). Isobel Gowdie also spoke of being fed beef when she met with the Queen and King of Fairy, another sign of the wealth of the Good Folk (Wilby, 2005). These descriptions all paint a picture of a world that is superior to the human one, flowing in wealth, happiness, and beauty in contrast to a contemporary earth in which the humans who saw these things lived in great poverty.

Travelling to Elfland can be achieved in several ways, some simpler than others. One Scottish man accused of witchcraft described going into Elfland by walking through an open door in the side of a hill, and other accused Scottish witches said they were conveyed there in the company of groups of fairies (Wilby, 2005). Some accused witches also described being taken from their bodies so that their spirits flew to the Otherworld for various fairy meetings, reflecting the wider Scottish idea that Elfland could be reached either physically or in spirit (Wilby, 2006; Goodare, 2020). Others claimed that they were carried off in gusts of wind or magically carried through the air (Henderson & Cowan, 2007). Tam Lin says he was brought to the Otherworld in the arms of the Fairy Queen who had snatched him up when he fell from his horse; Thomas the Rhymer describes a complex journey across a desert, fording rivers of blood, and beyond the land of living humans. The Fairy Queen in 'Thomas the Rhymer' describes the path to Elfland as beautiful and winding through fern-rich hills. When the narrator is returned from Fairy in the 'Wee Wee Man' it is through a mist which descends to separate them from the world the Wee Wee Man brought them to, indicating that mist, or specifically magical mist, may also be a route to and from Elfland.

As in other places the line between fairies and human dead is blurry in Scottish belief while also being distinct. There are beings among the Fairy throng who are clearly nonhuman or inhuman and who seem to exist outside of human society. The Fairy Queen is prime example of this, a being who is often connected to mythic or divine figures, compared in appearance to the Virgin Mary, and who exists outside human morality; she regularly engages in sexual acts with the human witches she interacts with – Andro Mann being a clear example – and offers help to humans in anecdotes and ballads as often and inexplicably as she harms them (Wilby, 2006; Goodare, 2020).

This distinction from humanity can also be seen in an account from *Fairy Faith in Celtic Countries* which claims the fairies could be heard singing:

> *Not of the seed of Adam are we,*
> *Nor is Abraham our father;*
> *But of the seed of the Proud Angel,*
> *Driven forth from Heaven.* (Evans-Wentz, 1911).

This is reiterated in a Scottish story of an elf mother trying to hide her infant to protect him from being used to pay the fairies' rent (discussed below) which says *"a mother's aye a mother be she Elve's flesh or Eve's flesh"* making clear that there was a distinction made between the two groups (McNeill, 1956).

In contrast we also find a range of humans tangled up with the fairies, both living ones like Tam Lin who was supposedly taken when he fell from his horse to dead ones like Tom Reid who appeared as a fairy familiar to Bessie Dunlop at the behest of the fairy queen (Wilby, 2006). While Tam Lin, in the ballad, is clearly a fairy man he seeks to return to human life, implying a fluidity between the two types of beings or at least that a human stolen while alive might be returned to the human world if the proper rescue was enacted. In contrast Tom Reid was a human man who was known to have died in battle and while he acts to guide Bessie Dunlop and keep her in line with the fairy Queens wishes he never (so far as we know) implies or asks to be rescued from the fairies, indicating that there was an understood difference between living and dead humans incorporated into the fairies. There also seemed to be a belief that living humans who associated with fairies or had a relationship with them were more likely to be taken into Elfland when they died. The implication being that for those humans Elfland would be a kind of afterlife which they would receive due to their connections to the Good Folk.

A unique belief found in the border areas was that Elfland didn't actually belong to the People of Peace but they rented it from the Devil, paying a tithe or kane [rent payment] to Hell on a set schedule. We see references to this in the 'Ballad of Tam Lin', 'Thomas of Erceldoune', and in accounts from at least one of the Scottish witchcraft trials of the 17th century. This idea is a product of syncretisation between older folk beliefs and Christian beliefs which place the fairies themselves as well as their land in a grey area between heaven and hell; while other cultures, like the Irish, see the land of Fairy as more neutral in Scottish belief Elfland is closer to Hell than heaven or even mortal earth and so the idea develops, particular in the Lowlands and border areas, that Elfland is properly a part of Hell but is rented out by the Good Folk to create the land of Fairy. According to this belief the fairies must pay their rent either every year or every seven years on Halloween by giving souls to Hell and this is used to explain the concept of changelings[3], so that the fairies steal humans in order to pay this rent without losing their own Folk in the process (Lyle, 1970). In some accounts the tithe is a literal tithe of 10% of the population while in others it is a single person. A story related by McNeill in *The Silver Bough* mentions an elf woman who hid her infant son in the cradle of a human baby so that he wouldn't be taken for the tithe, making it clear that humans weren't the only ones given. The oldest mentions of the tithe come from the area around Selkirk, and seem to have originally been unique to that area although it later spread, even finding a place in some modern popculture; for example, the tithe is referenced in the book and mini-series *Jonathan Strange & Mr Norrell* as if it were ubiquitous for all fairies.

The idea of the tithe to Hell might more generally tie into the idea that Elfland itself was a third path between Heaven and Hell, possibly meant to evoke the concept of purgatory (Henderson & Cowan, 2007). Although it could be argued that Elfland is an entirely unique concept it was at the least inserted into Christian thought as equivalent to limbo or purgatory, and may arguably have helped shape the ideas of purgatory during the 12th century. We find references to the idea of three paths or roads leading out of mortal earth in several ballads including 'Thomas the Rhymer' and 'The Queen of Elfin's Nourice', where the view of these paths is presented as a wonder that humans can't see unless it's revealed to them in those contexts by the Queen of Elfland.

Another uniquely Scottish concept, although one which has spread in modern fairy belief[4], is that of the seelie and unseelie courts which shape Elfland into two distinct factions. This belief grew from an older use of seelie as a euphemism for fairies more generally, with seelie meaning blessed, lucky, or fortunate. We find references to this usage into the 15th century but with no obvious moral implication; that came later in the 18th and 19th century when we start to see the idea of an opposing unseelie court comprised of the beings that are more overtly dangerous to humans. For example, in the 'Ballad of Tam Lin', version J, we see the seelie court referenced:

The night, the night is Halloween,
Tomorrow's Hallowday, our seely court maun ride,
Thro England and thro Ireland both,
And a' the warld wide. (Acland, 2003)

However, this seems to have no moral implications and is used simply to indicate the fairies more generally, as indicated by the fairies' actions throughout the ballad, from Tam Lin's collecting a toll from maidens at his well to the Fairy Queen cursing Janet for rescuing Tam Lin in the end. In the 'Ballad of Alison Gross', it is the 'Sely Queen' who appears on Halloween night to free the protagonist of the ballad from the curse he is under, while in the Legend of the Bishop of Saint Albois' a human woman is described as stealing goods and bringing them to the 'sillie wichtys' [seelie beings] and in the 'Ballad of Lady Mary O'Craignethan' it is a man of the seelie court who kidnaps the eponymous Mary, showing the ambivalent nature of the fairies even those labelled seelie.

By the mid-20th century the two court system was widespread in Scottish belief, enough that it is mentioned in McNeill's *Silver Bough* as an accepted facet of Scottish fairies. It is never clearly explained how this would impact Elfland more generally but the implication is that the fairies exist in two opposed groups, one which is somewhat more well inclined towards humans and one which is more malicious; although neither group was entirely benevolent. The unseelie were more likely to be malicious without a cause but the seelie would willingly harm humans if they were motivated to, although they generally would offer a warning to the erring human before acting (McNeill, 1956). The latter perhaps suggesting that unseelie was an alternate term for the Fuath, the Gaidhlig word for the group of particularly malicious fairy beings found in folk belief. This view should be understood as a fluid one, where a being might be perceived as Seelie in one account and Unseelie in another based on their various actions towards humans. A kelpie, for example, was generally understood to be dangerous and would be considered Unseelie, however, in some tales a kelpie might fall in love with a mortal and genuinely care for them, and in others might safely do farm work as long as they were kept away from the sight or scent of a body of water.

As we find in Ireland the fairies' government is a monarchy, as rev Kirk says: "*they are said to have aristocratical rulers and laws*" (Kirk & Lang, 1893). This idea is echoed by the accused witches who testified about meeting the Queen and King of Elfland or in some cases of the Queen seeking them out, an idea echoed in 'Thomas the Rhymer' where the Fairy Queen finds Thomas and kidnaps him to Fairy. Unlike monarchy, as we may imagine it elsewhere, the Scottish Kings and Queens of Elfland seem far more likely to engage with humans and even to wander in the human world on their own.

The King of Elfland is referenced in several Scottish folklore pieces, from 'Thomas of Erceldoune' to 'Alice Brand', but never given a name; rather the king is only ever referred to by his title. Accused witch Isobel Gowdie describes the King of Elfland as an elegant beautiful man. He is an obscure figure and appears as a being that is dangerous and mercurial, and very territorial of that which he considers his. In some sources he may be equated to the Devil, such as we find in 'Thomas of Erceldoune' where the Queen of Fairyland's husband and king is the Devil, who also collects the tithe to Hell, perhaps implying greater authority or perhaps representing an amalgam of different folk beliefs.

The Queen of Elfland, like her king, is also a figure that appears across folklore without being given a name. She is a less mysterious figure than the king and is given more characterization in the stories and ballads she appears in. In 'Thomas the Rhymer' she takes Thomas as her lover and in the same way, accused Scottish witch Andro Mann claimed to have fathered many children with the Queen, while Tam Lin claims it was the Queen who personally stole him away, connecting her intimately to humans. In 'Thomas the Rhymer' she is said to wear green velvet and ride a white horse with bells in its mane and tail.

Another monarch referenced in Scottish folklore is the Seelie Queen, who is mentioned in the 'Ballad of Alison Gross' as well as in some Scottish witchcraft trials. She is a nebulous figure, described as beautiful but also mercurial, likely to give aid but also potentially dangerous. It is quite likely that she is synonymous with the Queen of Elfland.

Nicnevin is claimed to be a Queen of Elfland, along with her unnamed King, in the works of Alexander Montgomerie and Sir Walter Scott and. Later folklore and modern belief place her as the Queen of the Unseelie court specifically which is in line with the descriptions given in the older sources which equate her to Hecate, a figure called the Gyre-Carlin, and describe her leading both witches and a parade of more dangerous fairies out on Halloween night[5].

End Notes
1. Elfland appears under a variety of spellings and forms, including Elf-land, Elphland, Elf Land.
2. There are additional terms in Gaidhlig that also mean a fairy hill including sìthean and brugh.
3. According to widespread belief across all Celtic language speaking cultures the fairies steal humans and replace them with a being called a changeling, which may be an inanimate object, a failing fairy infant, or an old fairy disguised with magic to look like the stolen human. Why they do this is unknown but many theories are offered including use as breeding stock for the fairies, wet nurses, entertainment, and because they covet the person.
4. We will discuss this in depth in Chapter 8.
5. The references to this predate the calendar change in the late 18th century so her particular night is now said to be 11 November, the old date of Halloween.

Chapter 4

Annwn

And he beheld a glade in the wood forming a level plain, and as his dogs came to the edge of the glade, he saw a stag before the other dogs. And lo, as it reached the middle of the glade, the dogs that followed the stag overtook it and brought it down. Then looked he at the colour of the dogs, staying not to look at the stag, and of all the hounds that he had seen in the world, he had never seen any that were like unto these. For their hair was of a brilliant shining white, and their ears were red; and as the whiteness of their bodies shone, so did the redness of their ears glisten. – First branch of the Mabinogi, trans. Guest

Also called Annwfn in older Welsh, the Welsh Otherworld is a complex place; the name is sometimes translated as Otherworld, sometimes as Underworld, and arguably has no good English language equivalent. In the Christian period Annwn would be conflated with Hell but this doesn't appear to reflect genuinely older folk belief (MacKillop, 1998). Dr Gwilym Morus-Baird breaks it down to: an 'very' and dwfn 'deep world' giving us 'very deep world' and describes Annwn as a deep aspect of our world, seeing it more directly connected to the human world than some other understandings of the Otherworld portray (Morus-Baird, 2020). Sims-Williams breaks down the etymology several different ways but finally settles more or less on 'under world' meaning a world that is beneath or under the human one, reflecting the concept found across Welsh myth and folklore of reaching Annwn by going down into the earth or beneath water (Sims-Williams, 2011). It is important, however, not to jump to associating the Welsh Otherworld via translation as the underworld with wider western European concepts of the underworld as the realm of the human dead.

Annwn is sometimes portrayed as a mysterious island that appears and disappears while other times, such as in the story of Arawn and Pwyll, as a land that is directly part of Wales but normally imperceptible or inaccessible. It is always a place that is both here and not here, both part of the mortal landscape and transcending it. As with the Irish and Scottish concepts the Welsh Annwn – or at least the entrances to it – are often anchored in physical locations in this world, sometimes islands or hilltops; unlike the Irish the Otherworldly islands in Wales are often inland ones, separated from land by fresh water rather than salt water (Kruse, 2018). It is important to note that while the previously discussed Irish concept of the Otherworld was a diverse realm of many individual and often different territories the Welsh is far more contiguous and may be described as one united place with a single king, although that kingship may at times be disputed (Sims-Williams, 2011).

As with the Irish an Saol Eile we find a variety of named places associated with Annwn which may be synonymous with it or may be specific places within it. We will discuss a selection of them here:

Caer Siddi – the etymology is uncertain but siddi is often related to the old Irish word sidhe, giving us 'fortress of the Otherworld' or something similar. It is possible that the use of this term reflects a borrowing from the Irish, and could indicate that the Welsh and Irish concepts of the Otherworld 1000 years ago was seen by those cultures as synonymous, although they were not identical and had important differences (Morus-Baird, 2020). As with most such places it goes by other names as well including those listed below, although how similar or distinct each is may be debated.

Caer Siddi has no sickness or old age, sweet music is heard throughout, and a fountain there flows with water that is more delicious than wine (MacKillop, 1998).

Caer Feddwid – fortress of intoxication.

Caer Wydyr – fortress fort. Also called Ynis Gutrin, glass island, it is ruled over by nine maidens and has been linked through folk etymology to Glastonbury (MacKillop, 1998). In this context it may be related to or the same as Avalon, discussed in the following chapter.

Caer Arianrhod – the home of the goddess Arianrhod and also often conflated with the constellation Corona Borealis. In the medieval poem Kadeir Kerritwen Caer Arianrhod is described as an island, surrounded by a river which separates it from the land around it and puts it into the category of an Otherworldly island (Kruse, 2018).

Annwn is inhabited by various types of beings but most notably perhaps the Tylwyth Teg and Plant Annwn. The Tylwyth Teg or 'Fair Family', are beings who may appear the size of children or much like human adults, who are described as physically beautiful, and ambivalent towards humans; the Tylwyth Teg love singing and dancing, and their dances create fairy rings (Briggs, 1976). As with other types of fairies the Tylwyth Teg are known to occasionally steal human children, sometimes as companions for their own children sometimes for other purposes. The Plant Annwn [children of Annwn] owe fealty to Gwyn ap Nydd, one of the kings of Annwn, are connected to lakes and include a range of specific beings including the Gwragedd Annwn [maidens of Annwn], Cwn Annwn [fairy hounds], and the Welsh fairy cows that live in lakes (Briggs, 1976).

As with the previous Otherworlds we've examined, Annwn is a monarchy, although unlike previous examples it doesn't usually have a named queen in folklore, although Creiddylad may be an option. Rather we find several kings associated with it who will be discussed here.

The King of Annwn is sometimes said to be Arawn and other times said to be Gwyn ap Nudd. Arawn is mentioned in the Mabinogi, specifically the first and fourth branches, as the King of Annwn while Gwyn is credited with that title in various stories and poems. A third king, Hafgan, is mentioned in connection to Arawn as another King of Annwn but he is defeated by the human Pwyll and gives his portion of rulership to Arawn.

Annwn appears as the ruler of an Annwn which exists side by side with human reality, encountering Pwyll in the first branch of the Mabinogi after Pwyll goes hunting and becomes lost following his dogs. Arawn is engaged in a battle with a rival, Hafgan, who is also described as a King of Annwn. In the first branch of the Mabinogi the human King Pwyll rides unwittingly into Annwn and encounters Arawn after driving Arawn's cwn Annwn – Otherworldly hounds – off a deer to allow his own dogs to take it down. Arawn is offended at what Pwyll has done and demands that the human repay him for the offense. To do this Pwyll must switch places with him for a year and a half, during which Pwyll will have to battle Arawn's rival Hafgan. Arawn advises Pwyll on how to win the battle, which Arawn has been unable to do, and when the time comes Pwyll successfully kills Hafgan who – before dying – cedes his portion of Annwn to Arawn.

According to Lorna Smithers, Gwyn ap Nudd means 'White son of Mist' and he can be traced back to the Iron age as a Brythonic deity (Smithers, 2014). Gwyn as King of Annwn fights against Gwythyr ap Greidawl for the hand of Creiddylad[1] every May Day for eternity and only the winner of the final battle would get Creiddylad. This arrangement was worked out by King Arthur who settled an ongoing dispute between the two by decreeing the yearly battle; some have speculated that Gwyn and Gwythyr represent seasonal kings of the Otherworld who trade of kingship, although the actual text doesn't entirely support this idea. In the tale of Culhwch and Olwen Creiddylad is engaged to marry Gwythyr when Gwyn kidnaps her; the two raise armies who fight each other. Gwyn wins but tortures several of Gwythyr's men who he has captured. Arthur eventually intervenes to settle the issue as related above. In that same text Gwyn is said to have been set in charge of Annwn to keep the 'devils' there contained. A 14th century invocation[2] to Gwyn in Latin calls him the king of the 'Kindly Ones' a euphemism for fairies.

There is also a reference to an obscure figure named Avallach or Afallach as the King of Annwn. This appears in the story of Urien and Modron, where Urien accosts a woman washing at a ford, but instead of being angry she thanks him because she is under a curse to wash there endlessly until she conceives a son by Christian man; she identifies herself as Modron daughter of Afallach and claims her father is the King of Annwn (Bromwich, 1963).

And Evens-Wentz recounts one Welsh source claiming that the king and queen were Gwydion ab Don and Gwenhidw, who has a castle in the stars named Caer Gwydion.

End Notes

1. Creiddylad may be Gwyn's sister according to some sources, although she is clearly playing the role of lover in this story.

2. *'ad regem Eumenidium et reginam eius: Gwynn ap Nwdd qui es ultra in silvis'* To the king of the Kindly Ones and his queen, Gwyn ap Nudd who is in that forest. Recorded in Lindahl et al. 2002. Eumenidium literally means kindly ones but is also a euphemism used for the Furies.

Chapter 5

Avalon

*'Sed et inclitus ille rex Arturus letaliter uulernatus est; qui illinc
ad sananda uulnera sua in insulam Auallonis'*
(The illustrious King Arthur too was mortally wounded; he
was taken away to have his wounds tended to the island of
Avalon)
Historia Regum Britanniae

Avalon or Ynys Afallach – isle of apples – from the Old Welsh
aballon meaning apple, also called by the Latin term Insulis
Avallonis in Geoffrey of Monmouth's work (MacKillop. 1999).
Avalon is described, like most Otherworlds, as a place of youth,
health, and celebration, and also one that is strongly associated
with both healing and epic heroes. It is mainly discussed in
various Arthurian works where it exists as a mystical land near
to or within Britain. The earliest references to Avalon appear
in the 12th century, but were later expanded on and in French,
English, and Welsh material as well as modern fiction. The idea
of Avalon was widely popular, with the first written text likely
reflecting older oral tales and leading to a wide array of literary
references and folk belief that extend into today.

Geoffrey of Monmouth is the first to write in detail about it in
both his Historia Regum Britanniae and Vita Merlini in the early
12th century, although it is unlikely he created the concept. He
connects Avalon strongly to King Arthur and Arthurian myth
more generally, as the place which Arthur's sword, Excalibur,

was forged and also the place to which Arthur was taken after being mortally wounded. He describes it thusly:

> *The island of apples which men call the Fortunate Isle (Insula Pomorum quae Fortunata uocatur) gets its name from the fact that it produces all things of itself; the fields there have no need of the ploughs of the farmers and all cultivation is lacking except what nature provides. Of its own accord it produces grain and grapes, and apple trees grow in its woods from the close-clipped grass. The ground of its own accord produces everything instead of merely grass, and people live there a hundred years or more. There nine sisters rule by a pleasing set of laws those who come to them from our country* (Parry, 1925)

From this we can gather that like other iterations of the Otherworld Avalon is a place without physical labour or illness and is a place associated with happiness and good fortune as well as healing. Avalon is entirely self-sustaining, a place which creates all that it needs from within itself and which offers an abundance not found elsewhere (Flood, 2015). Chaucer and d'Outremeuse both write of humans living among the fairies there, specifically Arthurian knights like Gawain and Oberon (Gawain's cousin, not the famed Fairy king), as well as other knights like Ogier the Dane. D'Outremeuse describes Avalon as a place of peace, eternal youth, and also of abstinence from sex (Green, 2016).

Although the beliefs around Avalon would change across the centuries and were heavily influenced by literary works Avalon itself exists in and influences folklore, and has from the beginning. Both Gerald of Wales and Gervase of Tilbury mention Avalon as a place believed in by the common folk, establishing its presence in folk belief during those periods and supporting a view that Avalon existed as such before Geoffrey of Monmouth's work (Green, 2000). It should be noted, however, that other scholars, like James Wade, disagree with this view and believe that Geoffrey was instrumental in forming Avalon as we know it.

The exact nature of Avalon and its geography is somewhat nebulous in older sources. Across history Avalon has been located in various types of places, including an island, a mountain, and beneath a lake, with no decisive agreement to its nature (Green, 2016). In many of the narratives around Avalon it is described as an island, even conflated by Garcia de Salazar with the Irish Hy Breasail. In contrast, however, de Baron describes it as a valley in western England. Thomas Mallory's famous Le Morte d'Arthur describes Avalon as an island several times and as a valley once, further muddying the waters. The early 13th century story 'Ogier the Dane' describes Avalon as a castle.

Today Glastonbury is often associated with Avalon and there has been much speculation that it represents the physical location of the Otherworldly realm, or perhaps a confusion between a physical place and a mythic one. Although now landlocked, prior to the 12th century Glastonbury was surrounded by a large marsh and could only be reached by bridge or boat (Mann, 2001). Gerald of Wales writing in the 13th century had this to say in his *De Prinicipis Instrucione* about Avalon:

What is now known as Glastonbury was, in ancient times, called the Isle of Avalon. It is virtually an island, for it is completely surrounded by marshlands. In Welsh it is called Ynys Afallach, which means the Island of Apples and this fruit once grew in great abundance. After the Battle of Camlann, a noblewoman called Morgan, later the ruler and patroness of these parts as well as being a close blood-relation of King Arthur, carried him off to the island, now known as Glastonbury, so that his wounds could be cared for. Years ago the district had also been called Ynys Gutrin in Welsh, that is the Island of Glass, and from these words the invading Saxons later coined the place-name "Glastingebury" (Thorpe, 2021).

While not conclusive proof that Glastonbury is Avalon it does show that the connection between the two places has been assumed for at least 800 years. There was also quite a famous claim made in 1191 by monks at Glastonbury that they had found the grave of King Arthur, linking both the stories and Arthur himself to the physical location (Green, 2000). While the claim was later debunked through an analysis of the evidence the monks had put forward – a cross which was proven to be contemporary to the claim not historic – the connection between the place and the idea of Avalon and Arthur remains strong today.

Rulers of Avalon are surprisingly diverse, particularly the range of named queens. While many people will think immediately of characters they are familiar with from modern re-tellings or popculture, we find the array across folklore more complex. Here we will discuss the queens and king associated with Avalon and whatever information we may have about them.

Geoffrey of Monmouth claimed that Avalon was ruled by nine sisters: Morgen, Moronoe, Mazoe, Gliten, Glitonea, Gliton, Tyronoe, Thiten and Thiton. Morgen, also called Morgaine, Morganna, or Morgan la Fey (Morgan the fairy) is probably the most well-known of the nine. Originally a distinct Otherworldly figure she was later framed as Arthur's sister or half-sister, slowly reworked over the centuries from a powerful fairy into a duplicitous human.

Argante is the Queen of Avalon according to a 12th century romance by Layamon (MacKillop, 1998). In that text, Layamon's Brut, Argante is described as the Queen of 'fairy elves' who were present at Arthur's birth and who later took him to the island of Avalon after he was injured, where its noted Argante was queen. She is described as the fairest of maidens and an elf, and it is said that she healed Arthur's wounds with magical draughts (Madden, 1847). This is a particularly Anglo-Saxon take on the story which reframes the Welsh and French fairylore of other versions into the elves of Anglo-Saxon lore.

Enfeidas is said to be the Queen of Avalon in a 13th century work by Heinrich von dem Turlin. She is an otherwise obscure figure. Avalon's ruler is generally referred to as the Lady of Avalon or Dame of Avalon in a late 13th century French work written in Venice (Larrington, 2006). It is unclear if this figure was known elsewhere by another name or only by this title.

Avallach is sometimes named as the King of Avalon, although Flood suggests that this is a later English insertion into the Welsh narrative. Elsewhere in Welsh mythology Avallach is said to be the father of Modron and a ruler of Annwn[1].

King Arthur was said in various sources to have been taken to Avalon after being mortally wounded in the battle. Many stories would later claim that Arthur had been healed, usually by Morgan la Fey, and remained in Avalon either by her side or as a king; the Gesta Regum Britanniae, for example, says that Morgan healed Arthur and he remains with her in Avalon. In other tales, however, Arthur was said to have gone into or been given rulership of an underground Otherworldly kingdom, from which he'd return when Britain was in its greatest need, while yet others suggested he had taken leadership of the Wild Hunt[2], itself strongly connected to the fairies in many places (Green, 2000).

End Notes

1. See the pertinent section in the chapter on Annwn.
2. There is also folklore which places Arthur in the form of a bird, a Chough specifically, or claims that he became a constellation (Green, 2000). Discussing those is somewhat outside the scope of this work but is worth mentioning as it further establishes Arthur's significance across folk belief.

Chapter 6

Fairy

Now in the olden days of King Arthur,
Of whom the Britons speak with great honour,
All this wide land was land of faery.
The elf-queen, with her jolly company,
Danced oftentimes on many a green mead
Chaucer, The Wife of Bath's Tale

The Otherworld is perhaps best known in English as the Land of Fairy, Fairyland, or simply Fairy, a name for it which we find in use back to at least the 14th century in the middle English form of Fayerie. As discussed previously this term comes from the older French and was used in English interchangeably for both the place and the beings who inhabit that place. I would suggest that the English understanding of Fairy and descriptions of it are an amalgam of the French material with existing Anglo-Saxon, Celtic, and Christian ideas, giving us a concept that reflects a fascinatingly diverse blend of beliefs. This blend of beliefs in turn has been a strong influence on the 20th and 21st century ideas about Fairy and so are important to understand as fully as possible.

This chapter will look specifically at beliefs from England, across the centuries, relating to the world of Fairy, discussing in places where those beliefs came from. Because of the way that these beliefs have formed we may touch on material here which is, strictly speaking, outside the Celtic language cultures but which nonetheless has been interwoven with them and is foundational in helping to form the English ideas about Fairy.

As Aisling Byrne points out in *Otherworlds: Fantasy & History in Medieval Literature*:

It is only after the Norman invasion that otherworld accounts begin to proliferate and their emergence in the twelfth and thirteenth centuries goes hand in hand with a widespread fascination with the marvellous that characterized the courtly writing of that period. (Byrne, 2016).

In other words, the English idea of Fairy doesn't appear in written accounts until relatively late and through the obvious influence of external cultures being incorporated into literature and then folk belief. Prior to this change in view accounts with Otherworldly beings, referred to then as aelfe, occurred within the confines of the human world, as experiences of the Other here rather than as journeys out of this world into another. When this perception shifts, we see narratives emerging around the world of Fairy, both in medieval romances as well as more humble literature.

Despite this merging and the later references to a discrete world of Fairy there remains a persistent idea that Fairy is also a place within the natural world. This is expressed through Chaucer's 14th century *Wife of Bath's Tale* where England is said to have once been *"land of fairy"*, in Shakespeare's 16th century *Midsummer Night's Dream* where the antics of Oberon and Titania play out within the same wood that the human protagonists are stumbling through. Dryghton's 17th century 'Nymphidia' places the fairies as insect sized beings who exist among flowers and beehives, rooted firmly in the human world.

The land of Fairy is encountered as both a place adjacent to or overlapping mortal earth, as we see in the Chaucer quote which opens this chapter, as well as a distinct place that must be journeyed to, as we find in 'Sir Orfeo', where Orfeo must travel through a split in a stone and three miles further to reach the land of Fairy. We find the same in the story of Reinbrun in the *Romance of Guy of Warwick*, wherein Reinbrun must travel through a dark wood, then a half mile into a hillside before reaching the wonderous land found within. Fairy is then both here and there and may be experienced by chance or through intent.

Fairy as a distinct reality is often described across the English sources as an idyllic, pastoral place, filled with gentle bird song and abundant fruit, often featuring grand castles or luxurious pavilions (Byrne, 2016). In the 14th century poem 'Sir Orfeo' the land of Fairy is described as a place of endless green pastures and forest, which was home to a great castle made of crystal and with rooms built of gold and jewels. In contrast to many other depictions of Fairy as sunless, the Fairy of Orfeo's tale is lit by a summer sun during the day and by the shining of the crystal castle at night which shone like the sun (Weston, 1914). A particular feature of the English Fairy is its abundant supplies of food and drink; while other views, such as the Irish, also make mention of the Otherworld as a place of feasting English stories emphasize this more usually along with the great temptation of that food or wine for the human (Byrne, 2016). Byrne points out, however, that this luxury and richness is contrasted by the horrors that exist side by side with the beauty, so that the experience of Fairy is never an unmixed one, never wholly beautiful nor wholly terrible. In Fairy there is never one without the other close at hand. The fairies exist in a morally neutral place, blessing those they favour but stealing humans and from humans without hesitation and in the same way we see them associated with both physical beauty and with maimed and mangled humans held within their world, juxtaposing beauty and cruelty in a way that defies the common stereotype of beauty equalling goodness (Wade, 2011). Fairy is, at its heart, a place of contradictions where the contrast between opposing forces illustrates the beyond-human nature of the world.

It is generally understood that Fairy is inhabited by fairies, however, as with other iterations of these beliefs, things are more complicated than they first appear. While it is true that many of the beings found across folklore relating to Fairy are non-human beings that seem to come from and exist primarily outside humanity there are also those among the fairy throng who were once human. In some English folk belief King Arthur resides in Fairy[1], sometimes alone or with his most trusted knights but in other accounts with his entire retinue; there is even some folk belief that sees a version of the Wild Hunt – the Familia Arthuri – as the collection of Arthur's people who ride the night (Green, 2016). Similarly folk belief across the medieval and early modern period often conflated some groups of human dead with the inhabitants of Fairy, making it a place that people who died in specific ways might go, particularly those who died by violence. The epic poem 'Sir Orfeo' describes this well in the passage where the protagonist has first entered the land of Fairy:

And in sooth he beheld a fearsome sight;
For here lay folk whom men mourned as dead,
Who were hither brought when their lives were sped;
E'en as they passed so he saw them stand,
Headless, and limbless, on either hand.
There were bodies pierced by a javelin cast,
There were raving madmen fettered fast,
One sat erect on his warhorse good,
Another lay choked, as he ate his food.
Some floated, drowned, in the water's flow,
Shrivelled were some in the flame's fierce glow;
There were those who in childbed had lost their life,
Some as leman, and some as wife;

Men and women on every side
Lay as they sleep at slumbertide,
Each in such fashion as he might see
Had been carried from earth to Faerie.
(Weston, 1914)

This idea is echoed as well in several of the fairy ballads, including 'Tam Lin' and 'Alice Brand', where there is reference to a human being taken by the fairies either after being killed or in the moment of death; Tam Lin as he fell from his horse and Alice's brother when he was struck down in battle. Indeed, the wider idea of fairies stealing humans away to joining them in Fairyland is a very old one, attested to in English material at least as far back as the 14th century *Fasciculus Morum* which criticized belief in fairies[2] and the idea that fairies can take men and women away and change them into *"other beings"* as nothing more than demonic delusions (Green, 2016).

Despite this widespread folklore around the human dead in the land of Fairy, we must be careful not to assume that either humans in Fairy are dead or that Fairy itself is equivalent to a human afterlife. There is abundant evidence of some human dead being seen later in Fairy or among the Fairy throng but there are also accounts of humans taken alive or prior to the moment of death. Indeed, as Richard Firth Green says in *Elf Queens and Holy Friars* (p 160) *"We should be careful about seeing Fairyland...as simply a land of the dead."*. Green goes on to point out that in folk belief figures like King Arthur who may be found in Fairy are not dead but emphatically alive and able to return to the human world. In other stories humans taken by force into Fairyland may escape or be returned to their former lives, something we see in 'Sir Orfeo' as well as the 'Ballad of Thomas the Rhymer', and go on to live relatively normal lives. The penchant for fairies to steal living humans away to Fairyland is mentioned at least as far back as the 13th century in

Thomas of Cantimpre's *Bonum Universale de Apibus* wherein the author discusses the way that "demons" [read: fairies] may take a living person and leave behind a substitute which the person's family buries and mourns.

Besides the humans and former humans who make up the population of Fairy there are also many other types of beings who are not and never were human but owe their existence entirely to Fairy. The kings and queens of Fairy (discussed at the end of this chapter) are examples but we can also look across the range of English folk belief to the array of spirits described under the term. Even in 'Sir Orfeo' there is a seeming divide between the human dead seen there and the fairy cavalcade seen by Orfeo entering the Fairy king's castle, with the human dead still bearing the marks of their violent deaths and displayed almost as trophies in the castle contrasting with the active and unmarred host and monarchy (Spyra, 2015).

One of the more interesting and earliest English accounts of Fairy come to us from the account of the 'Green Children of Woolpit', a 12th century pseudo-historical story of events said to have happened in Suffolk. The story is told in two main sources, the late 12th century *Historia rerum Anglicarum* by William of Newburgh and the early 13th century *Chronicon Anglicanum* by Ralph of Coggeshall. The story generally goes that while a group of men were in a field harvesting the crops two strange children – green skinned and wearing clothing of an unknown material – wandered out of an area full of old pits[3]; the children didn't speak any familiar language and would eat nothing at first but raw peas. Eventually they did learn to speak English[4] and relayed that they had come from a strange foreign land. In William's account he claims the children said they were from a place called St Martins which knew neither sun nor moon but was a Christian country and that they didn't know how they had come to Woolpit beyond being enchanted by the sounds of bells ringing; in Ralph's account they claim that their homeland is in perpetual twilight and all people there are green-skinned, and that they wandered into a cave following the sound of bells and out near Woolpit but were struck helpless by the sunlight and temperature. While the accounts differ in various ways both agree that the children's original home existed without sunlight or night and that the children found themselves unable to return to it after arriving in Woolpit. This is more widely in line with beliefs about Fairy which often describe it as existing in a kind of perpetual gloaming and talk of people wandering unwittingly between realms. The details of the children not speaking any known language and wearing strange clothing of an unknown material are also in line with wider beliefs[5] as is their inability to find their way back to their home.

In English belief the land of Fairy is usually understood as a monarchy which is ruled either by a Queen, King, or both together. This Fairy monarchy is a reflection of the English monarchy and indeed several of the literary portrayals of this structure which have been absorbed into wider belief were written as satires on the English monarchy, such as Dryghton's 'Nymphidia', or as propaganda for it, such as Spenser's 'Faerie Queene', so that the concepts of Fairy monarchy and human monarchy are much more closely intertwined than what we may see elsewhere.

Most often the King of Fairy in folklore and related material is nameless, referred to only by his title, as we find in 'Sir Orfeo', however, there is at least one notable exception. Oberon is perhaps the best known of the English kings of Fairy, gaining renown through Shakespeare's work. Shakespeare is not, however, the first to write about or mention Oberon, as he appeared several centuries earlier in the French *Les Prouesses et faitz du noble Huon de Bordeaux*, although there he is not a king but an elf who inhabits a forest. The name Oberon goes even further back to the Germanic Alberich, literally 'elf king', found in German folklore and the 13ᵗʰ century Nibelungenlied. After Shakespeare, Oberon would continue to be referenced as an English fairy king in both literature and poetry, paired with various fairy queens. In the 17ᵗʰ century 'Robin Goodfellow: His Mad Pranks and Merry Jests' Oberon is named as the father of Robin Goodfellow by a human woman, an idea perhaps supported by Shakespeare's claim in *A Midsummer Night's Dream* that Oberon was fond of taking human lovers. It should be noted that in Huon of Bordeaux, Oberon is half-human, the son of Julius Caesar and a fairy woman, although in later sources he is generally understood as one of the immortal fairies himself (Green, 2016).

As with the king of Fairy the queen is often nameless, described by her title when she appears in stories or ballads. It is slightly more common to see an unnamed fairy queen acting alone than to see a fairy king, and this may speak to a wider inversion of human social norms at play in Fairy. That said there are a range of named fairy queens found across English literature, magical grimoires, and folk belief, and we will examine several of them here.

Titania may be a form of Diana and appears as the Queen of Fairy alongside her king, Oberon, in Shakespeare's *A Midsummer Night's Dream*. Shakespeare seems to have created her as such, although she may have deeper folkloric or mythic roots under a different name. Nonetheless, after being popularized in *A Midsummer Night's Dream*, Titania is often given as the name of the Queen of Fairy in England and is known widely as such in modern media, from fiction to games.

Although somewhat less well-known, Mab[6] is another of Shakespeare's fairy queens, appearing in *Romeo and Juliet* where she is described as the fairies' midwife and said to be the size of an insect. In the 17ᵗʰ century Drayton follows on from this in his 'Nymphidia' by relating a tale of insect sized fairies including fairy Queen Mab and her husband Oberon. She would continue to appear in fiction in the role of a queen across the ensuing centuries and continues to be depicted as such today.

Spenser's epic 16th century poem 'The Faerie Queene' gives us Gloriana as the Queen of Fairy, an Otherworldly monarch who is – at best – a thinly veiled fairy version of Queen Elizabeth I of England, but who has been forwarded as a fairy queen since.

Proserpina is mentioned as a fairy queen in Thomas Campion's early 17th century *Book of Ayres*, where he includes a poem 'The Fairy queen Proserpina', in which he entreats lovers to be good to each other or else risk Proserpina's anger, saying that to those who make their lovers cry:

The fairy queen
Will send abroad her fairies everyone,
That shall pinch black and blue
Your white hands and fair arms

Proserpina also appears in Dryghton's 'Nymphidia' as a power equal to Pluto who commands the bickering fairy knight, Pigwiggen and fairy King Oberon to cease their quarrel.

We also find accounts of fairies and fairy queens in some of the grimoire material, most notably accounts gathered in the *Book of Oberon*. The main queen found here is named Sybil or Sibilia. She initially appears in a 15th century work by Antoine de la Sale where he describes a fairy world ruled by Sybil which is idyllic, full of beautiful scenery and noble characters, although it should be noted that de la Sale was writing of fairies in the context of visiting the Greek Sybil's cave, applying his understanding of fairies to that location (Green, 2016). She also appears in two ceremonial magic spells, referenced as the queen or empress of all fairies (Harm, Clark, & Peterson, 2015).

End Notes

1. Often interchangeably referred to as Avalon, which was discussed in depth in the previous chapter.

2. Referred to in that text as elves, which the author says is the term 'in our native tongue'. This, of course, reflects the wider fluid usage of elves and fairies as synonyms found across the beliefs.

3. These would be the pits from which the town of Woolpit got its name, old structures that according to the story were called 'Wolfpittes' and had been dug a defence against wolves. This is a legendary explanation for the pits rather than a true history, but folklore attributes Woolpit as the location where the last wolf in England was killed.

4. To be clear, early middle English not to be confused with modern English.

5. There are, of course, a wide range of explanations that have been offered for the origins and nature of the green children, from aliens to feral children to immigrants who became lost and suffered from a medical condition which discoloured their skin (Clark, 2018).

6. Often conflated with the Irish Medb [Meave] it should be noted that there is no foundation for a connection between the two: their mythology and folklore is very different and etymologically their names are unrelated. The idea that they are identical has become increasingly popular but should be viewed as a modern concept.

Chapter 7

Christian Influences

Up, Urgan, up! to yon mortal hie,
For thou wert christen'd man;
For cross or sign thou wilt not fly,
For mutter'd word or ban.
The Ballad of Alice Brand

The relationship between fairies, the world of Fairy, and Christianity is a complicated one, but one that has undeniably shaped later beliefs across folklore and into spiritualities like theosophy and the new age movement. In the earliest accounts we find no references to human religion affecting the Good Folk and we find an Otherworld that is most often a fantastic reflection of the human world, filled with feasting, fighting, and trysting; in later stories, however, the Otherworld has been tempered and softened (a process which has notably continued into the 21st century). This tempering seems to be the effect of centuries of Christian influence on both the folk beliefs as well as the wider popular culture. Along with this restructuring of Fairy we also find increasing references to fairies who are averse to Christian signs and prayers, either through animosity or jealousy[1] as well as fairies who are themselves practicing Christianity or seeking Christian salvation. The blending extends as well to the way that the stories are told: when Thomas the Rhymer first sees the Queen of Elfland he mistakes her for the Virgin Mary, and in their respective tales both Orfeo and Graelent initially mistake Fairy for Heaven, details which would have given context to a Christian audience for the things being described. To understand why that is and how it came to be we must look at the history of how these beliefs crossed and integrated.

As Christianity gained popularity across western Europe the views and understandings of fairies and Fairy were affected. The new religion sought to place these older, persistent beliefs into a framework that aligned with a Christian cosmology and so during this period we see evolution and adaptation of these beliefs. To understand the world of Fairy today we must, perforce, understand the affect that Christianity and Christian cosmology had on the folk beliefs relating to it. This is, however, a difficult conversation to have, not because we don't have a lot to discuss or information on the subject, but because it can be a challenge to decide exactly which was influencing which. We certainly do see a lot of similarity between Fairy and Christian concepts of purgatory as well as older depictions of paradise, but is this because Christianity influenced the folk beliefs or because the folk beliefs influenced Christianity? The academic view tends to assume that the first option is the default, that it is always Christianity that influences what's around it. However, the conversation is more complex than this and I think it would be more accurate to argue that each belief influenced the other. This argument is somewhat of a moot point, however, as we have no pre-Christian material for the cultures we are discussing and therefore no way to be certain about the pre-Christian belief; we must ultimately conclude that the beliefs have been syncretic across at least the last thousand years. There are, however, certain threads that we can trace out from the wider concepts and we will be discussing those here.

One of the main arguments towards the Christian influence on the understanding of the Otherworld is that it is described across medieval sources in ways that mirror or directly copy

Christian descriptions of paradise. As Byrne says: *"...the line between more 'secular' otherworlds and the afterlife of Christian belief is often blurred in medieval narratives."* (Byrne, 2016). It is impossible to know if this is merely a case of Christian scribes using the language they were familiar with to describe an existing concept or if they influenced the depiction based on their own understanding of what a pleasant non-earthly realm must be like. Moving forward into this chapter it is important to understand though that not all details relating to these later understandings of the Otherworld reflect purely Christian ideals as we still see a world of Fairy that is full of battle, sex, and hedonism past the 17th century. Nonetheless Christian cosmology has had its effect, particularly in taming the sharp edges of the Otherworld and in placing it as a world more distinct and distant from the human world than previous understandings. This reflects the way that medieval Christians understood reality as composed of this world and the other world, two distinct places in which souls would reside (Dinzelbacher, 1986). There was also considerable blurring between the concept of the Otherworld and both the underworld and the land of the dead (Byrne, 2016). This idea of a distinct other world inhabited by the dead blended with folk beliefs about an ancillary or attached Otherworld inhabited by fairies to create a syncretic belief which was then further blended into Christian cosmology.

We see this syncretism keenly with the Irish Otherworld and the beings within it, who persisted into the modern era despite attempts to disempower them across a millennium and a half. Through this process the older concepts and beliefs had to be fitted into the new and this was done, most often, by stretching the Christian beliefs to include Fairy and fairies. The fairies become a kind of fallen angel, too good for Hell but too bad for heaven, who are perpetually concerned for their own salvation, a thing from which they are exempt. There are various folktales that tell of a fairy or group of fairies who approach a priest asking about whether they will get into heaven or not and are usually told they won't because they lack a soul or lack the red blood of humanity; the reaction to this is usually poor and sometimes explains why some fairies are malicious towards humans. Fitting the narrative of fairies as a kind of angel the land of Fairy itself becomes a sort of unofficial purgatory, a place that is neither heaven nor hell but a liminal zone between them.

An example of this Christianization may perhaps be found in the 'Green Children of Woolpit' (discussed previously) who according to William of Newburgh claim to have come from St Martin's land, a place where Saint Martin was given special reverence. While it has also been suggested the green children may have been human the idea that they were fairies has seeped into the wider culture to a degree that eminent scholars like Katherine Briggs and Diane Purkiss counted them among the fairy throng (Clark, 2006). Based on this presumptive fairy nature the land they called home, St Martin's Land, has also in some places been assumed as a name for the world of Fairy – at least one portion of it – and further connected to the harvest festival of Martinmas (Clark, 2006). Briggs herself suggests a possible connection between these fairy children, St Martin's Land and the land of the dead, which may in itself reflect the strong connection in Christian thought between Fairy and purgatory. Much of the wider discussion around this is speculative, however, at the least it reflects the way that Christianization impacted fairy belief across the last eight centuries, that it was acceptable to folk belief to connect the green children and their foreign home, with its perpetual twilight, to a Catholic saint and further to accept the idea that the people of this subterranean land would have a special dedication.

Another aspect of the Christianization of Fairy that can clearly be seen is the change from emphasizing it as a place where sex was commonly engaged in to one where abstinence was an ideal. In many of the earlier Irish texts like Echtra Nera or Echtra Laeg mac Crimthainn we see humans who adventure into a Saol Eile taking lovers or being given spouses and in the 'Ballad of Thomas the Rhymer' the fairy queen takes Thomas as her lover. In contrast we find later tales like the Echtra Thaidg which directly blend Christian elements in, including calling the Otherworld one of four paradises founded by four daughters of the Biblical Adam, and describe it, under the name Inisderglocha, as a place of chastity where lovers exchange nothing more intimate than affectionate looks (Byrne, 2016). Jean d'Outremeuse's 14th century *Ly Myreur des Histors* describes Avalon as a place of abstinence, something that was meant to imply its ideal nature, reflecting wider Christian mores of the time. In this way the ideas around Fairy were altered from a place of sexual joy[2] to one of abstinence, effectively making Fairy into a watered-down Heaven and moving the understanding of it towards the Christian view of purgatory, which began to develop as such in the 11th century.

John Carey discusses the main Christian approaches to the Otherworld seen in the older Irish material in his book *A Single Ray of the Sun* where he describes two methods within medieval Christianity of dealing with these concepts, specifically around the Irish Gods who would become the Aos Sidhe [people of the fairy hills]; he suggests that the church scholars either demonized what they encountered in stories or reduced them to merely human figures (Carey, 1999). This is played out in relation to the world of Fairy itself in the way that terms which may be applied to it are also ambiguously applied to human locations considered beyond civilization such as Norway[3] or the Isle of Man, rendering the Otherworld mundane.

As this influence spread and became more pervasive we find tales of fairies who are deeply concerned with their own salvation through the church and who engage in Christian religion themselves[4]. There are accounts in Ireland of fairies who were helpful to humans, particularly aiding in the harvest, until they ask a priest or he tells them of his own accord that they will not be saved on Judgement Day because they are not human; upon hearing this the fairies leave in a rage and refuse to aid humans again afterwards (MacNeill, 1962). In contrast in the School's Collection at Duchas.ie there is a story of a man who was invited into a fairy rath, into the Otherworld, to attend the christening of a fairy baby. The 14th century French fairy woman Melusine mourns that her husband's betrayal of her trust has cost her a chance at Salvation, implying that had he kept his promise to her she would have been saved at Judgment Day (Green, 2016). Many of the Scottish ballads reference Christianity in various ways, such as the quote which opened this chapter where a man who was stolen by the fairies and transformed into one of their number is sent out to deal with human interlopers because he had been a Christian and was therefore immune to Christian prayers and the sign of the cross. In 'Huon of Bordeaux' the death of Oberon is accompanied – at Oberon's request – by Christin prayers and signs, which resulted in the fairy king's soul being ferried to Heaven by angles as Huon watched (Green, 2016). In all of these stories we see Christian beliefs integrated into folk belief and reflected through stories of Christian fairies or fairies who want to be Christian.

Descriptions of the world itself also show signs of this influence over time and in various places. Around Selkirk in Scotland the land of Fairy becomes a sublet of Hell, separate from but intrinsically belonging to the Devil, and a place for which the fairies must pay rent. In contrast in the tale of Reinburg in the *Romance of Guy of Warwick*, Fairy is described in hyperbolic terms as a wonderous paradise of beautiful landscapes, sweetly singing birds, fabulous buildings, and immortality even for humans brought there. This presented a problem for medieval writers who fashioned a land of Fairy that was a reflection of paradise and had to find ways to show that despite its similarity to Heaven in was inferior. In 'Tam Lin' and 'Thomas the Rhymer' this is achieved by adding a hidden infernal risk to Fairy so that humans who dwell there may find themselves offered up to pay the fairies rent to Hell. The 15th century Irish tale *Altram Tige Da Medar* presents the Otherworld as a beautiful and abundant place but one that is filled with contention and prejudice in contrast to the perfect peace and welcome of Heaven. In the English literary tales of Fairy, it is shown as an idyllic place but one which lacks the passion and vitality of the human world, a pale reflection of earthly life which is ultimately inferior to what a living human can find by remaining on earth.

Ultimately how much or little influence Christianity has had on the concepts of Fairy is difficult to judge. We have no pre-Christian sources for fairies within the Celtic language speaking cultures and can only attempt to make comparisons with pre-Christian sources from related cultures and from there make educated guesses. There are certainly some things, such as those discussed in this chapter, which are more blatant or obvious or were explicitly described within a Christian context within the texts – the Echtra Thaidg describing it as one of four paradises founded by the daughters of Adam, for example. But ultimately there is a syncretization which occurred across the medieval period that has had wide ranging effects in how Fairy is understood today, and which must be understood as both a foreign influence on the material and an intrinsic part of it now.

End Notes

1. While we will touch on the subject here it is worth noting that quite a bit more can be said about fairies and Christianity than can be discussed here without digressing too far from the focus of the chapter.

2. It should be noted that the fairies themselves were seen as having a deeply sexual nature, so much so that incubus was commonly used to gloss fairy in texts and there is a

strong tradition of fairy lovers (of both genders) across Celtic and English material. Richard Firth Green discusses this in depth in his *Elf Queens and Holy Friars*.

3. Keeping in mind, of course, that the Norse raided and even settled parts of Ireland, creating a very contentious relationship between the two cultures.

4. Interestingly, this parallels middle eastern beliefs around the jinn, who may be antagonistic to Islam or may practice it themselves, across folk belief.

Chapter 8

Modern Fairy

The green hill cleaves, and forth, with a bound,
Comes elf and elfin steed;
The moon dives down in a golden cloud,
The stars grow dim with dread;
But a light is running along the earth,
So of heaven's they have no need:
O'er moor and moss with a shout they pass,
And the word is spur and speed
The Faerie Oak of Corriewater

Fairy has gone through many changes in popular culture across the centuries and while some may have the idea that Fairy today is a homogenous concept in truth it is as diverse as ever, if not more so. The older threads of cultural folklore remain, adapted to a modern world, and various new understandings have come into being created from sources as widespread as popular fiction, mysticism, movies, and new spiritual movements. Each of these views spreads and impacts how both individuals and groups imagine the Otherworld and in turn how new generations will understand it.

The world of Fairy in artwork and in modern fiction is most often shown through an anachronistic lens, that is its depicted as a place that exists outside of time and stuck as it were in the human medieval period. People hear the fairy ballads of the 17th century, read fairy folklore of the 18th and 19th century, and this image of Fairy as a place caught in history is established. That isn't the entire picture, however, in fact isn't the picture those stories were meant to convey at all; however, the way that popular culture and many 21st century people understand the world of Fairy is shaped from that understanding and equally from fiction. We must also take into account the powerful impact of both theosophy and the new age movement in shaping the current wider ideas about the Otherworld. In this chapter we will explore several of these newer views, their roots, and how they both weave together and contradict each other.

It is important here to discuss two major influences on modern perceptions of 21st century fairies and Fairy: theosophy and the Victorian era. While theosophy began in the late 19th century it has had a lasting impact on popular culture and neopagan fairy beliefs which have come afterwards, as has the wider reshaping of Fairy and fairies by popculture during the Victorian era. The Victorian era writers and artists reshaped fairies into twee winged children and theosophy pigeonholed them as elemental spirits and beings without tangible reality. Theosophical writing of the time, particularly by Helena Blavatsky, strayed from the wider understandings of fairies as powerful, sometimes physical beings to describe them as a sort of undeveloped soul or spirit which was incapable of physical form and which was bound to one particular element in which it acted as an invigorating force (Blavatsky, 1975). The world of Fairy became the world of the four classical elements and the interrelated human world as manifest through plants and minerals. This view then influenced occultists who came afterwards, for example, WB Yeats, who started in Theosophy before joining the Golden Dawn, and by dint of this influenced later neopagan views drawn from 19th and 20th century sources. At roughly the same time the wider popular culture of the Victorian era was moving into a view of fairies that was both infantilized and disempowered; much as the Tudor and Edwardians in England had reduced fairies to insect sized because of their infatuation with the miniature so the Victorians made fairies an intrinsic part of the human natural world (Silver, 1999, Purkiss, 2000). The world of Fairy in this view was an increasingly green space and fairies themselves were pulled from a mystical Otherworld to take up residence in gardens and flower petals. These two views, working together, have been carried forward into the way that many people today understand both the Otherworld and its inhabitants, and should be understood as an underpinning to most of the following views we will be exploring here.

Fairy as Natural World

One aspect of the Victorian influence can be seen in the way that some have come to view the human natural world as the home of fairies, in place of an Otherworld. This view can be seen particularly in children's media including movies like *Fern Gully* and *Epic*, which situate the homes of the fairies as very much within the human world but outside of human perception. Examples of this in modern belief can be found across several anecdotal accounts in the 2018 Fairy Census, such as S18: *[I thought it was fairy] because it occurred in a natural environment. The being looked real and of this earth, but out of place in my reality.* (Young, 2018).

Fairy as Higher Evolution

While Blavatsky was adamant that fairies existed as less evolved souls who were working towards human incarnation there have been various authors since the 1980s who have taken the opposite tack, blending fairy beliefs with new age ideas around ascended masters and spirit guides. Several books have been published in the last 20 years that purport to speak for the Good Folk themselves, usually referred to as the Sidhe[1]. A selection of these books[2] work from the view that fairies are more highly evolved than humans and exist now to aid humans in becoming better humans and better souls. The world of Fairy is understood differently by different authors using this approach, from John Matthews description of the home of the 'sidhe' as a world like the human one but more vivid and enspirited, to David

Spangler's description of Fairy as a place defined, in some ways, by the perception of the human experiencing it and which is filled with things that exist beyond human perception and where magic replaces technology[3] (Matthews, 2004, Spangler 2014). In both of those examples fairies themselves are more highly evolved beings who seek to guide humans and whose world appears to be an adjacent dimension to ours.

Fairy as Afterlife

A popular modern iteration of Fairy, particularly among neopagans, is the idea that the world of Fairy is synonymous with the human afterlife. This concept weaves together a variety of historical ideas across cultures, blending the older Irish, Scottish, and Welsh beliefs about some of the dead going to live among the fairies with the later Christian descriptions of the place as an idyllic paradise, and 20th century wiccan ideas about the Summerlands as a place where souls rest before rebirth. Instead of existing as one possible place that various dead humans might end up, this view sees Fairy as the place where all humans go after death, before rebirth into the human world, and argues that living humans are spirits of Fairy. As witch Veronica Cummer puts it in her book *Elfhame's Children*: "*...when you are here in this world, you are essentially a Faery incarnated in a physical body. When this body dies, you are then released back to Faery.*" (Cummer, 2018).

Fairy as Utopia

A now common view of the Otherworld which has been shaped by both Christian influence and later Victorian views is that of Fairy as a utopia. While it is true that older versions of Fairy often emphasized it as a place that was preferable to and more peaceful than the human world – hence its allure to mortals taken into it – it was also clearly established as a place that wasn't perfect or exempt from violence. It was, in short, an idealized version of the human world but one which retained some of the risks and dangers of human life. In contrast the Otherworld as it has come to be expressed through this lens took on aspects of the Christian ideas around heaven blended with an idealized view of non-corporeal reality creating a place that is idyllic and utopian, a place of peace and plenty without risk or dangers, and without the boredom or longing for earthly life which coloured the earlier Christian interpretations. This view is oftentimes expressed by authors.

One aspect of the impact of popular culture on beliefs around Fairy can be found in the way that the Scottish fairy courts are often seen as universal, that is that the world of Fairy is one united place which is divided into two groups, the Seelie and Unseelie. In some views the Unseelie are the 'bad' fairies in contrast to the 'good' Seelie, but it has become increasingly common across popculture to understand the Unseelie as the better of the two, with the Seelie being more duplicitous and secretly vicious while the Unseelie are honest and straightforward (Daimler, 2021). The two groups are sometimes referred to today as the Bright and Dark courts or as the good and bad fairies, both of which tend to have inherent moral implications; another alternative is the summer and winter courts which avoid any implied morality to the groups but do emphasize one as friendlier than the other. This adaptation seems to have been drawn from fiction, particularly urban fantasy, of the 1980's and 90's which brough the idea of the two courts to the mainstream public but described it as a universal feature of Fairy government rather than the folkloric view that the courts were human perception based on fairy interactions.

A modern change in the view of Fairy that can be traced to theosophy is the idea that Fairy is an intangible place that has no physical existence or reality and can only be reached through mental exercises or dreams. This is, of course, in sharp contrast to the older beliefs that positioned Fairy as a physical location that could be walked into and in which a human could have tangible experiences including conceiving or fathering a child, for example. While it's true that the older views were fluid and often treated Fairy as both physical and potentially non-physical, suggesting that the two states could and did exist simultaneously or interchangeably the modern view favours Fairy as entirely and immutably incorporeal. In other words, it sees Fairy as non-physical and unable to be physical. This reflects the late 19th century theosophical view of fairies as entirely intangible beings, and of the world of Fairy as either incorporeal or woven into the human world.

Having had a brief look at some of the modern understandings of Fairy that have been born out of the 19th and 20th century popular culture we will now turn to looking at some other views of Fairy in the 21st century that are based in anecdotal accounts and address the question of whether Fairy itself is modern or antiquated. Through this lens we are looking at living beliefs of Fairy today specifically among neopagans, and to a lesser extent some new age authors. These are modern sources which are vocal about their thoughts and experiences, often outside of an older cultural framework, and whose views further act to shape the wider understanding of Fairy.

Across a range of folklore, we find stories of humans who were brought into Fairy and in those stories what they describe isn't an ancient society or older architecture but things that would have been similar to what they knew in their own homes, towns, and cities only often described as grander or more luxurious. At some point as folklore moved into a written genre as well as the older oral stories the idea of Fairy as a place that looked very much like earth only more magical and richer changed into this idea of an antiquated and historic place, because the written sources were fixed in time rather than adapting as the oral sources did[4]. And yet many modern people who have experiences with Fairy in dreams, visions, or trance work find themselves in Otherworldly places that mimic the modern human world, showing that despite the wider popular view Fairy as contemporary to the human world seems to remain true in some anecdotal accounts.

One particularly interesting question that is being asked by many people about Fairy as we understand it today is where exactly modern human technology might fit in. For some people envisioning Fairy means picturing a bucolic and idealized rural land or even wilderness. Fairy becomes a projection of all the romanticized notions of nature that people nurture. On the other hand, for some people, Fairy is and always has been a fantastical reflection of the human world as it is, including both wilderness and cities, farms and palaces, and showing humans the luxury and abundance they dream of.

While I have yet to see any folklore around the ideas of fairies taking or borrowing modern human technology there is an old trope around fairies borrowing human tech, most often hand mills, when that technology was new. Briggs discusses several examples of this in her *Dictionary of Fairies*, suggesting that the fairies are borrowing technology they themselves don't possess, which at the least implies that the Good Folk are willing to take and use human tech when it benefits them.

While not situated in Fairy itself we do have some few accounts of fairies – of various types – either using human vehicles or being seen driving their own versions of such. There is a notable account from early 20th century Welsh folklore, mentioned in Brigg's *Dictionary of Fairies*, which describes a pixie taking the bus to fetch a midwife and then bring her back via bus to a stop near where the labouring woman was. In 1979 six primary school students in England said they saw what they described as gnomes riding in small cars, who proceeded to chase the children out of the park they were in (Young, 2022). These examples demonstrate the way that fairies are perceived in some contexts as existing within the modern human world, and at least support the possibility that a modern Fairy would also have contemporary features.

In this final section we're going to examine some modern aspects of Fairy that have been expressed in anecdotes and what is sometimes referred to as personal gnosis[5]. These experiences and perceptions are not universal to modern fairy encounters or current views of Fairy but they do reflect views and experiences relevant to modern Fairy within specific demographics. I believe that these are pieces of wider universal concepts, although I will note that there are also modern experiences that include encountering beings in old fashioned dress and visiting places that seem right out of a history book or fantasy story.

The Train Station

A place that I have encountered in dreams and which several people I am acquainted with have also mentioned experiencing is what I choose to call the Train Station. For those who have described experiencing it the Train Station appears much like a large human train station but may be notably built with bronze rather than steel or feature tracks that go in impossible directions (Daimler, 2023) It has also been described as a transitory place that acts as an interchange between destinations within Fairy and a quick way to travel from one place to another (Heath, 2018). It seems to exist as a type of transfer point or hub connecting different places within Fairy or perhaps different worlds within that wider concept.

A Fairy City and Commercial Spaces

Across a range of modern anecdotes, we find references to Fairy having cities although the nature of these places seems to depend somewhat on the human relaying the story. David Spangler describes a city in Fairy via his channelled source Mariel as:

...concentrations of creativity, art, culture, and spirit.... We have our skyscrapers just as you [humans] do, but they are towers of thought and energy. They are aspirations made visible. (Spangler, 2014).

In contrast, others have experienced cities in Fairy that are very similar to human cities and places that are typical work or commerce locations; John Beckett describes an office building in Fairy with a typical human-world style meeting room (Beckett, 2018). I have dreamed of a city in Fairy that is exactly like a city in the human world, including a trendy outdoor café (Daimler, 2023). Catherine Heath discusses the modern aspects of the Otherworld in various ways including as a large supercentre type store and a large school, as well as a bus depot (Heath, 2018). In these examples we find a Fairy that is in many ways a mirror of the human world, although always with an Otherworldly twist, an aspect that is beyond human or beyond the possibilities of this human world.

Housing

While we may be inclined to picture houses in the world of Fairy as either castles or antiquated cottages, several people have described personal experiences of Fairy which featured modern housing. John Beckett, describing a dream of Fairy related it this way:

...a very ordinary 20th century American house. When I went outside I saw lawns and trees and driveways and all the other things you'd see in a residential neighborhood." (Beckett, 2018).

I have also had experiences of houses in Fairy that seem like modern cabin style homes, with running water, bathrooms, refrigerators, and stoves – although I'd note there didn't seem to be any obvious electricity and I can only guess at what was powering the modern conveniences I saw.

Fairy is a complex place and what we know about it runs a gamut between older tales of medieval or even Iron Age places to very modern ones with all the features we would expect in the current human world. While I wouldn't suggest that the world of Fairy now is only reflective of a modern human world, I think we must include modern reflections into an understanding of Fairy in order to have the fullest view of what it is and can be. Across the history of the folk belief accounts have always shown Fairy to be a place that is both deeply foreign and achingly familiar, a place that is like the human world but also unlike it, so it follows that we would find modern accounts to continue to be in line with this. It should also be noted that across the accounts Fairy is often similar to the contemporary human world of the story teller or slightly antiquated which has continued today, and that all accounts are unavoidably filtered through the lens of the storyteller, so that what we hear is the best description they can give based on their own experience. The result is a complex picture of Fairy that is, in most ways, very similar to what we might find in trying to describe the human world.

As we move to wrap up this chapter, I would like to touch on modern concepts around the government of Fairy and its rulers. It is more difficult in this context to include all possibilities because of the fluidity of modern beliefs and the speed and ease with which they are influenced by fiction, particularly television and books, however, it is worth mentioning the most popular ideas to be found. For many people Fairy remains a monarchy, although who rules that monarchy varies widely, reflecting all of the older beliefs as well as new ones. The names chosen for these universal rulers often draw from English material blended with Scottish, viewing Fairy as a place divided into Seelie and Unseelie but ruled by Oberon and Mab, or sometimes alternately one group is ruled by Titania and the other by Mab. It is also often put forward in modern contexts that Fairy itself is one cohesive place which exists under either a single set of rulers or a pair based in the court division. The more strongly new age view, as expressed by Matthews or Spangler, tend to favour either a loose leadership system or an egalitarian one, which reflects the wider view of that approach which sees Fairy as more utopian and evolved than humans.

End Notes

1. I will note here that a differentiation must be made between the Irish Aos Sidhe as found across myth and folklore and the beings referred to as 'Sidhe' within these texts as the two are markedly different and in many ways contradictory to each other. The 'sidhe' being channelled in the books referenced here should be understood as unique spirits in contrast to the Irish Aos Sidhe.

2. It should be noted that the community of people who engage in this approach is fairly small and also generally acquainted with each other in one context or another. While there are diverse opinions and viewpoints expressed through channelled material it is also common for people sharing a wider philosophical view who are friends with each other to produce similar material. It is for the reader to decide why that occurs, but such shared belief forms the core of the view of fairies as higher evolved beings.

3. For example, Spangler says that the 'sidhe' travel the stars not with mechanical aid but using the powers of their minds and spirits.

4. A notable exception to this may be the 'Ballad of Tam Lin' which has more than a dozen historic variations recorded but has continued to be adapted into the 21st century, including versions that place the characters in the modern world. The 1970 movie *Tam Lin* directed by Roddy McDowell is one example while 2008 the spoken word piece 'Tam Lyn' retold by Benjamin Zephaniah is another. Both anchor Tam Lin as a contemporary tale while retaining the themes or tone of the original. There are also multiple novelizations with contemporary settings including Catherine Storr's *Thursday*, Annie Dalton's *Out of the Ordinary*, and Pamela Dean's *Tam Lin*.

5. Personal gnosis, sometimes also labelled as UPG – unverified or unsubstantiated personal gnosis – is a term found across neopagan and related communities, used as a shorthand for knowledge that a person has due to a spiritual experience, dream, trance, or similar. This may perhaps be distinguished from anecdotal material in that an anecdote reflects an experience the person has had in a conscious, tangible context while personal gnosis often relates to knowledge obtained by a person in an altered state or dream.

Chapter 9

Through the Mist – Finding Fairy

And he went on a little further, till he came to an old woman in a grey cloak, and he asked her if she knew where the Dark Tower of the King of Efland was. "Go on a little further," said the hen-wife, "till you come to a round green hill, surrounded with terrace-rings, from the bottom to the top; go round it three times "widershins", and each time say: "Open, door! open, door! And let me come in."
– Childe Rowland

Up until this chapter this book has been focused on the various folklore about Fairy across the Celtic language speaking cultures and related areas which has contained within it small hints and suggestions for actual engagement, if one is so inclined. In this final chapter I want to offer some ideas for how to put the previous information into a practical context. For those whose primary interest is in the folklore think of this as the active side of those beliefs; for those who are interested in the active side this is a guide to the ins and outs of it all. In what is often called the 'fairy faith'[1] it is impossible to separate these two aspects, belief and practice, and both form a cohesive whole. The beliefs are the foundation of the practice and the practices give active purpose to the beliefs. It is in the spirit of that union of belief and practice that I offer the following chapter, outlining folk belief around how one would reach Fairy, survive there, and escape back to the human world again.

A Folklore Guide to Entering the Otherworld

Many people believe that the world of Fairy exists only a breath away from the human world, separated by a metaphorical veil or a magical mist, and may be wandered into or out of by the unknowing. This may be one way to understand it but there are also stories which describe the Otherworld clearly as a place that can be sought out and reached through specific means. Here we will discuss that aspect of things, since I can't offer any practical advice on how to wander in accidently. There are several ballads and story motifs that discuss methods of arrival in Fairy, which I'll be referencing here alongside the general folklore.

Moving Counter Clockwise

In the ballad of Childe Rowland the protagonist's sister initially disappears into Fairy after circling a church counter clockwise. Later in the story the protagonist himself gains entry into a fairy palace by circling it three times counter clockwise. It's understood that going counter clockwise or 'withershins' is moving against the sun and is the direction of the Good Folk themselves. Further to this idea an old Irish idiom for the fairies found in *O'Davoren's Glossary* is *'arna gentib impadhas tuaithbil'* [the people who turn against the sun] linking the Irish Aos Sidhe to the idea of counter clockwise movement, and implying it is part of their nature (Stokes, 1862). The idea here then is that moving counter clockwise, especially around places associated with the Good Folk can act as a means of opening up the entrance to Fairy.

Through Stone

In several stories including 'Sir Orfeo', the Echtra Nera, and some versions of the borrowed midwife entrance to Fairy is achieved by going through an opening in a boulder or cliff face, or entering a cave amid rocks. In these accounts we find the idea that Fairy is underground merged with the idea that it is a separate world, with the human passing through stone and into the darkness of the earth only to emerge into a unique world that is not within the earth but elsewhere. Although I should note that in some accounts the human is still within a cave but is misled by Fairy magic to perceive it as a grand space or other world, nonetheless in other stories it is clearly established as existing outside human world reality. There are a multitude of versions of the borrowed midwife tale, but in several we find midwives who are brought to Fairy by specific means, often riding on a horse behind a man they don't realize yet is a fairy, passing between stones and through tunnels or caves; their destination is also often a cave. Before you go wandering into caves and crevices it is also worth noting in these stories the human is invariably either travelling with a fairy who brings them there or is following a group of fairies that they have seen going into the place.

With an Escort

The most common way we see humans entering Fairy, across all the cultures and accounts, is with a fairy escort. The human is taken out of the human world and into the world of Fairy by either a single fairy or a group, and often brought to a meeting or to see the Fairy Queen. In folklore this is usually accomplished after the fairies show up and summon or abduct the human; in modern witchcraft and spiritual practices this may also be the case although we find accounts of those who go with a fairy guide who they have invoked or asked to take them.

Fairy Rings

While it has become a trend on social media to see people talking about fairy rings as portals into Fairy this is actually a very new concept. The folklore around fairy rings as portals is from the 21st century and, of course, doesn't hold up to actual experience based on the number of people jumping into them then complaining they are still on earth.[2] However, fairy rings do have a connection to Fairy and its inhabitants and there is folklore about people stepping into rings of mushrooms or dark or dead grass only to face consequences for doing so which might include being stolen away. Generally, when this happens it is not because the ring is a portal but because it is filled with invisible fairies merrily dancing who seize the human when they step across the boundary. Sometimes the person is forced to join the dancing and either[3] dies of exhaustion or leaves in the morning to find that a decade or century has passed. In some few accounts, however, the person disappears never to be seen again and was assumed to have been kept by the fairies who took them to the Otherworld. It is that final context which makes fairy rings a possible way to enter Fairy, although obviously a particularly dangerous one.

Off the Map

In prose and poetic versions Thomas travels to Fairy via a complex journey which involved crossing a desert where *"living land was left behind"*, fording rivers of blood, into a place without sun, moon, or starlight. Obviously not a general method that would be used, but the idea of a complex journey is worth noting here, at least in consideration of some of the more esoteric approaches we'll discuss below.

I would like to note one other method mentioned in folklore which would fall into the category of methods that can't be done intentionally but which nonetheless I'd like to discuss. Although obviously not recommended or a method one could likely do intentionally there are multiple accounts of people who reach fairy after getting lost and unintentionally wandering out of mortal earth. 'The Fairy Dwelling on Selena Moor' is a good example of this from Cornish folklore, where a drunk man rides his horse through what should be familiar territory only to find himself suddenly in an unknown place, which he describes as *"strange"* and *"so crowded with trees that he had to alight and lead his steed"* (Bottrell, 1873). Eventually he wanders into an orchard where he finds a group of "undersized" people and one woman who he had previously been in love with but who had died several years prior; she tells him not to eat or drink anything nor to kiss her or he will be trapped in the world of the 'small people' as she is. While not an intentional method it should be kept in mind as a way to enter Fairy anyway.

Other Means of Reaching the Otherworld

In contrast to those options which focus on physical entry, although not in contradiction to them, we also find that it's possible to reach Fairy through other means including dreams, trance, and what may be termed spiritual journeying. This reflects the dual nature of the place as both physical and non-physical and reflects the folklore which has always allowed for non-physical or spiritual means to reach Fairy.

Dreaming

It has been a long-standing belief up to the late 19th century that it was possible for beings of the Otherworld to communicate with humans in dreams and that it was possible for humans to travel to the world of Fairy the same way. Dreams were believed to have a reality to them that could include interacting with spirits, traveling out from one's body, and even being physically injured (Bitel, 1991). This view of dreaming allowed for a person to have fairy encounters or experience Fairy while still remaining physically in their bed, or wherever they were sleeping. Katherine Briggs recounts such an experience in her *Dictionary of Fairies* where she tells of a man who fell asleep on a hillside, travelled to a Fairyland, lived there for several years until breaking a prohibition and was banished, and woke up in the same hillside only minutes after falling asleep.

Trance

In Irish belief trance is a common means of both perceiving fairies and being taken to their world. Irish mná feasa [wise women] were sometimes thought to fall into trances where they would communicate with the Good People or go into the Otherworld (Ó Crualaoich, 2006). There are also numerous accounts of people who fell into trances, sometimes for years, who were thought to be in the world of Fairy (Evans-Wentz, 1911; Wilby, 2005). Ann Jeffries of Cornwall who was reputed to have a close relationship with the fairies first encountered them when she fell into a trance state and was brought to their world by a group of them (Buccola, 2006). These trances can be involuntary but can also be entered into at will by some people, and represent a method by which the person's soul was taken or sent out from the body.

Journey (Voluntary Trance)

A more modern practice used to reach the land of Fairy is spiritual journeywork, wherein a practitioner intentionally sends their spirit outwards and (in this case) travels to the Otherworld. Some modern anecdotal accounts mention this method being used and it may be viewed as a kind of 20th and 21st century folk practice. While the methodology is modern the concept it's based on is older and might be said to look to stories from Scottish witchcraft trials of witches who left their bodies behind to journey outwards to Fairy in spirit. Suggestions for how to accomplish this can be found across an array of modern material including work by Lora O'Brien, Lee Morgan, or Chris Allaun to name a few.

Surviving Fairy

Getting there is one thing but the real issue will come with how to act once you arrive, so the next logical step in discussing the practices is including a rough survival guide for those travelling in Fairy. Think of this less as hard and fast rules and more as general guidelines that will be situation specific. I will include the why behind the what to hopefully help you all better understand when to apply a rule and when to ignore it. Many of these could be expanded in culturally specific ways but as some of those ways are contradicted in other cultures, I am trying to stick with things that are generally seen as common across the entire range of beliefs.

1. Don't eat any food or drink anything – there is a long-standing prohibition across most fairylore that one should never eat or drink anything while in the realm of Fairy, or indeed while in the human world if it is being offered by a being of that world. The general belief is that to eat the food of fairies is to be irreversibly bound to them and their world. We see a wide range of anecdotes centred on this idea, usually featuring a human who has encountered a group of fairies and been invited or inveigled to join them, been offered food or drink, and is then cautioned by a human among the group (often recognized as a recently deceased community member) not to take the offered meal. The warning always includes the explicit message that if the food or drink is accepted the person will not be able to leave and return to the mortal world or their family. In the 'Ballad of Childe Rowland' the protagonist is advised to *"bite no bit and drink no drop"* when he goes to Fairy to rescue his sister if he wants to succeed and return again to Earth with her. There are some exceptions to this, particularly in situations when the food is being offered by one of the monarchs of the Otherworld, but overall, this is one of the most consistent prohibitions we find.

2. Be careful who and what you trust – Fairy is a place where appearances really are deceiving and that which seems the safest and most trustworthy is often the most dangerous, while those things that seem more dangerous sometimes are not. One needs to be especially discerning when dealing with this world and careful not to make assumptions.

3. The issue of time – another of the main constants of belief across cultures is the idea that time moves different in Fairy than it does in the mortal world. This time difference seems to be something that the Good Folk themselves have some ability to judge or control whereas humans find themselves at the mercy of its flow. There are countless stories of humans who are brought into the world of Fairy for what seems like a few hours or a night only to return to the human world and realize that years or even decades have in fact passed. For example, in the story of Niamh and Oisín, Oisín goes to live with Niamh in the Otherworld for what he believes is three years. He eventually starts to long to see Ireland and his family again and eventually persuades Niamh to let him go for a visit although she warns him not to touch the earth. When he returns to Ireland, he finds that rather the three years he experienced in Fairy 300 years have passed and all the people he once knew have died; and, of course, he slips off his horse and falls to the ground, immediately aging and soon dying as those missed years catch up to him. People who dance in fairy rings often find themselves stepping out at dawn into a world that is decades or a century beyond when they entered the ring. Many people who have had modern experiences with Fairy have also reported odd slips of time similar to this, where

the person believes only a small period has passed only to find out later that actually a much longer amount of time went by.

4. Watch your words, and everyone else's too – the folk of Fairy are notoriously tricksy and prone to semantics so it is especially important not to make any assumptions about what you feel is implied in things that are said and look only at what is actually said. There are numerous examples of humans who were tricked through verbal deceptions not because the being in question lied but because the human assumed a meaning to the words that wasn't there; for example, a story about a man who is asked by a fairy to promise he can have *'what stands behind this building'* and the man agrees assuming the fairy means the apple tree behind his house when in fact it is his wife (or daughter in other versions) who is standing there unbeknownst to him (Briggs, 1976).

5. Treat it as real – one thing that is consistent across folk belief and into modern experiences, although it is downplayed or ignored in the more new age based approaches, is the idea that what happens in Fairy even if it occurs in a dream or vision is just as 'real' as our waking reality. An example of this is found in folk accounts of witches who travelled out in spirit and were injured and when confronted the next day the injury that the spirit acquired is seen on the person's flesh (Lecouteux, 2003). The belief here is that what happens to the spirit will be mirrored in the body reflecting the wider belief that dreams and trance-journeys are as real as the waking world; although this belief has waned across the last century, largely due to the influence of psychology which places dreams as dialogue within the mind, it was a standard concept prior to the 19th century

(Bitel, 1991). Ideally one who is – or believes they are – interacting with Fairy should treat the experience as they would one in the waking world.

Getting Home Again

Once you have gone and done whatever it is you need to do – or want to do – the final step is, of course, getting back again safely. In some sources, like the 'Wee Wee Man' or 'Thomas the Rhymer', return from Fairy is facilitated by the Good Folk themselves who choose to send the human back. This is often accomplished by an instantaneous return to the place the person began. In other accounts returning involves retracing one's journey, effectively go back exactly as you came in. We see examples of this in the Borrowed Midwife stories where the midwife is brought back along the same route she was brought in. In the case of dreams or trances the human wakes up or returns to normal consciousness which acts to pull them out of Fairy, sometimes immediately and other times through a journey process where they trace their way back to their body.

Now it is worth concluding this chapter by looking at folklore around how a person might be rescued from Fairy, in a case where they were taken there unwillingly or are unable to leave on their own. This is a complex subject, and it should be understood that while rescue from Fairy is theoretically possible it is difficult and not always entirely effective. More than one account of a person stolen and rescued back mentions that the human is never entirely themselves again or in the worst-case wastes away and dies.

In some stories a person is rescued from Fairy when another person goes in to retrieve them, although it is never quite that simple. In 'Sir Orfeo' the eponymous hero rescues his wife from Fairy after she is abducted by going to the castle of the Fairy King and playing such sweet music that the king offers him any reward that he names; he, of course, chooses his wife. In 'Childe

Rowland' the protagonist's two older brothers proceed him in trying to rescue his sister from Fairy but he succeeds where they failed by carefully following Merlin's instructions to strike the head from anyone who speaks to him – including at the end his sister; this is a test which his brothers failed and although he is reluctant once he does strike the image of his sister his real sister is freed along with his brothers. In these examples a rescue can be achieved but only if the rescuer either wins the stolen person away from the fairies or can break their enchantment.

Other accounts speak of humans rescuing those stolen into Fairy when the stolen person emerges, however, briefly, back into the human world in the fairies' company. In the case of changelings[4] rescue may be achieved in some accounts by going to the closest fairy hill and waiting for the stolen person to emerge with the fairy cavalcade then snatching them from their horse. After rev Robert Kirk died mysteriously on or near a fairy knowe his cousin had a vision where Kirk told him he had been taken by the fairies but could be rescued if an iron knife was thrown over his head when he appeared at his son's christening – although this wasn't accomplished and he remains, so they say, with the fairies. Those stolen away by the slua sidhe [fairy host] can be rescued by throwing an iron knife at the host, or tossing up a handful of sand/dirt or item of clothing while yelling 'that is mine this is yours'. And 'Bald's Leechbook' discusses burning Mugwort to release a person from fairy enchantment.

The practices associated with going to, being in, and escaping Fairy are complex and varied. I have only offered a brief overview here but I encourage people to read or listen to the folklore to learn more and find the fuller range of examples. Despite the depth of the subject, I do hope that this chapter has helped provide a basic working knowledge of the subject that people can pair with the beliefs.

End Notes

1. Fairy faith is a name used by sociologists in the late 19th/ early 20th century for the group of beliefs and practices around fairies. It is not, of course, the term used by people who hold these beliefs or follow these practices, but it has become somewhat common in wider usage outside academia. Based on this English term in the late 20th century Catholic priest Seán Ó Duinn coined the Irish language term creideamh sí to refer to the specifically Irish versions of the beliefs and practices.

2. I am being slightly facetious here, but there is a noticeable trend across social media of such jokes. I've seen them in various forms, although I'm still unclear on what the person thinks would happen to them if they were taken. My impression is its nihilistic humour, but of a more dangerous sort than I'd personally recommend.

3. In fairness I will note that there are accounts in some French folklore of people who entered a fairy ring, dance, and leave unharmed in the morning.

4. Changeling folklore is vast and complex; I cannot touch on it in any depth here, however, I have written about it in my book Aos Sidhe.

Conclusion

Sed dicunt non per diabolum, sed pulchrum populum, nec diabolo didicimus nec ei credimus sed pulchro populo. Summa Predicantum, 1586
(They say it is not the work of the devil but of the fair folk for we haven't learnt it from the devil nor do we believe in him but from the fair folk.)

The subject of fairies waxes and wanes in popularity across the years but one constant is the way that humans are perpetually drawn to the world of Fairy and its inhabitants. By any name the world of Fairy is always separated from but intrinsically linked to the human world and the beings within it exist in a complex symbiosis with humanity and with the earth. Within this book we've looked at some of the oldest sources for the world of Fairy, traced the beliefs around it across various Celtic language speaking cultures, and looked at how these beliefs manifest in the modern world, as well as taking a look at what folklore might tell us about practical interactions with that reality.

Humans have been seeking Fairy for as long as we have stories of fairies – the oldest Irish language tale of the Good Folk tells of a young man who is wooed by a fairy woman and ultimately leaves this world to go with her to her own (Daimler, 2022). Indeed, the word itself as we established at the opening of this book does double duty, both a term for the beings and for the world they come from. We cannot separate out the one from the other, any more than we can separate the desire to find Fairy from human imagination and dreams. It is a place that calls to us, a place that is simultaneously deeply foreign and achingly familiar, a place that has existed one step sideways from our reality – apparently – since the beginning.

The subject is a complex one, in part because beliefs about the Otherworld exist as both unique cultural expressions and amalgams of those expressions, as both historic folklore and modern personal gnosis. None of these views is wrong and none fully encompasses exactly what the Otherworld is, rather every view and every understanding of Fairy builds on others, expanding or refining existing ideas to create constantly changing and evolving belief system. Much like the human world the world of Fairy is the sum of all of its parts, and much like the human world its diversity and expressions and cultures are vast and difficult to summarize. And much like the human world everyone will have their own opinions and perceptions of it. To fully define or understand Fairy would be to fully define and understand the human world; no matter how much we seek to compress and simplify the idea it will always be too immense to fully comprehend.

In this book we have looked at what the Otherworld is, various understandings of it in specific cultures, how it has been influenced by Christian cosmology, and how it exists and is understood in the 21st century, which has hopefully helped readers gain a stronger understanding of all of these complex subjects. This single book has its limits though and readers are strongly encouraged to keep diving deeper as much more could still be said about it both from a folklore perspective as well as from an experiential perspective. For those who are intrigued enough to want to go further there are two main options in line with those perspectives: study the folklore and explore the experiential accounts.

To better understand what Fairy is, by any name, you need to read the old stories and listen to the folklore. These are for all intents and purposes the maps that have been shaped by centuries of belief and shared experiences. We can find these accounts across Irish, Scottish, Welsh, and related folklore as well as French and English fairy beliefs. We can also find more by looking at modern stories and accounts of Fairy, although caution should be used here to separate newer folklore from what was explicitly created as fiction – for example, you will find people discussing Fairy through the lens of role-playing games and novels which has its place in the wider understanding of folklore but, in my opinion, needs to be understood within its context rather than taken as older or cultural belief.

Irish sources can include storytellers like Eddie Lenihan as well as modern Irish people who write about the folklore and stories such as Jenny Butler, Lora O'Brien, David Halpin, Shane Broderick or Anthony Murphy. A website called Duchas.ie is another good resource to look at as it contains a vast array of recorded beliefs from the early 20th century.

Scottish sources might include work by Julian Goodare, Emma Wilby, or Lizanne Henderson, all of whom have explored Fairy through the lens of academia, as well as looking across the Scottish ballads such as: 'Tam Lin', 'Thomas the Rhymer', 'The Queen of Elfin's Nourice', or 'Alice Brand'. Another possible source is the work of Sir Walter Scott.

Welsh sources in Fairy can be more limited unless one speaks or reads Welsh but I'd suggest looking at the work of Mhara Starling, Lorna Smithers, and Dr. Gwilym Morus-Baird for a better understanding there. English sources on Fairy may include authors like Mark Norman, Simon Young, and John Kruse. For Cornish my own personal go-to is Siân Esther Powell who does the Celtic Myths & Legends podcast (among other social media).

The other thread that has to be followed here in order to better understand the subject is practical experience. This is a muddier subject and readers will find a huge array of often contradictory material out there, from those who experienced fairies as tangible human-like beings to those who relate to fairies as almost imperceptible energy beings. However, all of these are important across the wider study of the subject and all provide small pieces of the full picture we seek to understand. The Fairy Investigation Society is a great resource for this aspect, particularly their Fairy Census which catalogues modern anecdotal accounts.

Any journey into Fairy, even a purely intellectual one, starts with a single step, a choice to walk into the mist or follow where the stories lead. This book is, at best, only a single step forward. Truly understanding Fairy is the effort of a lifetime.

Appendix A

Pronunciation

In this appendix I want to offer a pronunciation guide for some of the Irish and Welsh terms used in this book. These are only rough pronunciations and I encourage everyone who is interested to research further, preferably by checking with native speakers. However, this should provide at least a basic understanding of how these words should sound.

An Saol Eile – uhn Sehl Eh-leh
Annwfn – An-oh-ven
Annwn – Anoon
Aos sidhe – ace shee
Arawn – Ahr-ow-n
Caer Arianrhod – Ky-er Ah-ree-uhn-rhoth
Caer Siddi – Ky-er Sid-ee
Daoine sidhe – Theena shee
Emhain Abhlach – E-wen Av-lahk
Gwyn ap Nudd – Gwyn app Neath
Mag Mell – Mahg MehL
Manannán – Mahn-ahn-awn
Plant Annwn – Plahnt anoon
Sidhe – shee
Slua sidhe – sloo-uh shee
Tír fo Thuinn – teer fuh Hoon
Tír na mBan – teer nuh Mahn
Tír na mBéo – teer nuh M-ay-oh
Tír na nÓg – Teer nuh Nowg
Tír Tairngire – Teer Tahrn-gih-reh
Tylwyth Teg – Tehlooth tayg

Bibliography

Acland, A., (2001) *Childe Rowland*. Retrieved from https://tam-lin.org/stories/Childe_Rowland.html

— (2003) *Child's Notes on Tam Lin*. Retrieved from https://tam-lin.org/library/child_s_notes.html

— (1998) *Alice Brand*. Retrieved from http://tam-lin.org/stories/Alice_Brand.html

Allen, J., (1952) *North-East Lowlands of Scotland*

Askew, R., (1884) *Bye-Gones, Relating to Wales and the Border Countries*

Beckett, J., (2018) *The Otherworld in a Dream – 4 Things I Learned*. Retrieved from https://www.patheos.com/blogs/johnbeckett/2018/06/the-otherworld-in-a-dream-4-things-i-learned.html

Beveridge, J., (2014) *Children into Swans: Fairy Tales and the Pagan Imagination*

Bitel, L., (1991) *In Visu Noctis: Dreams in European Hagiography and Histories, 450-900, Histories of Religions vol. 31*

Blavatsky, H., (1975). *Elementals, Collected Writings*. Retrieved from https://www.theosophy.world/resource/elementals-hp-blavatsky

Bottrell, W., (1873) *Traditions and Hearthside Stories of West Cornwall, vol 2*. Retrieved from https://www.sacred-texts.com/neu/celt/swc2/swc216.htm

Briggs, K., (1976) *A Dictionary of Fairies*

— (1978). *An Encyclopaedia of Fairies: Hobgoblins, Brownies, Boogies, and Other Supernatural Creatures*

— (1978) *The Vanishing People: Fairy Lore and Legends*

— (1967) *The Fairies in Tradition and Literature*

Briggs, K., and Tongue, R., (1968) *Folktales of England*

Broderick, S., (2019) *The Evolution of the Irish Otherworld*. Retrieved from https://irishfolklore.wordpress.com/2019/07/26/the-

evolution-of-the-irish-otherworld/?fbclid=IwAR2cMFGxlrm6XP
szCeevs4PMQ4GMGQmw3tINE5LsebPXiAobcYqB1DYuk8o

Bromwich, R., (1963) *Trioedd Ynys Prydein*

Buccola, R., (2006) *Fairies, Fractious Women, and the Old Faith: Fairylore in Early Modern British Drama and Culture*

Buchan, P., (1828) *Ancient Ballads and Songs of the North of Scotland*

Burns, R., (1786) *Poems, chiefly in the Scottish Dialect*. Retrieved from https://www.scottishcorpus.ac.uk/cmsw/burns/

Byrne, A., (2016) *Otherworlds: Fantasy & History in Medieval Literature*

Campbell J., (1902) *The Gaelic Otherworld*

Campbell, J., (1854) *Transactions of the Ossianic Society*

Campion, T., (1618) *The Fairy Queen Proserpina; Classic & Contemporary Poetry*. Retrieved form https://www.poetryexplorer.net/poem.php?id=10024238

Carey, J., (1999) *A Single Ray of the Sun: Religious Speculation in Early Ireland*

Child, F., (1882) *The English and Scottish Popular Ballads*

Clark, J., (2006) *Martin and the Green Children*. Folklore 117

— (2018) *The Green Children of Woolpit*

— (2022) Online lecture '*The Green Children of Woolpit: the true old fairy mythology?*'. https://folklore-society.com/event/the-green-children-of-woolpit-the-true-old-fairy-mythology/

Cummer, V., (2018) *Elfhame's Children: the covenant of witch and faery*

Daimler, M., (2021) *Unseely to Anti-hero: The Evolution of Dangerous Fairies in folklore, Fiction, and Popular Belief*. Retrieved from https://www.academia.edu/49049249/Unseely_to_Antihero_The_Evolution_of_Dangerous_Fairies_in_Folklore_Fiction_and_Popular_Belief

— (2022) *Through the Mists*

— (2023) *21st Century Fairy*

Dalyell, J., (1801) *Scottish Poems of the Sixteenth Century*

Davies, S., (2007) *The Mabinogion*

De Beaumont, (1783) *'Containing Dialogues between a Governess and Several Young Ladies of Quality Her Scholars'*, The Young Missus Magazine, 4th ed vol 1. Retrieved from https://babel. hathitrust.org/cgi/pt?id=hvd.rsmcti&view=1up&seq=1

Dinzelbacher, P., (1986) *The Way to the Other World in Medieval Literature and Art*

Dobs, M., (1929) *Altram Tige Da Medar; Zeitchrift für Celtische Philologie vol. 18*

Erickson, W., (1996) *Mapping the Faerie Queene: Quest Structures and the World of the Poem*

Evans-Wentz, W., (1911) *The Fairy Faith in Celtic Countries*

Flood, V., (2015) *Arthur's Return from Avalon: Geoffrey of Monmouth and the Development of the Legend.* Arthuriana, vol 25, no 2. Retrieved from https://www.jstor.org/stable/24643472

Ford, P. (2008). *The Mabinogi and Other Medieval Welsh Tales*

Goodare, J., (2020) *'Emotional relationships with spirit-guides in early modern Scotland'*, The Supernatural in Early Modern Scotland

Gray, E., (1983) *Cath Maige Tuired*

Green, C., (2000) *'But Arthur's Grave is Nowhere Seen': Twelfth-Century and Later Solutions to Arthur's Current Whereabouts; Arthuriana.* Retrieved from http://www.arthuriana.co.uk/n&q/return.htm

Green, R., (2016) *Elf Queens and Holy Friars*

Guest, C., (n.d.) *The Mabinogion.* Retrieved from http://www.maryjones.us/ctexts/cadgoddeu.html

— (n.d.) *Culhwch and Olwen.* Retrieved from http://www.ancienttexts.org/library/celtic/ctexts/culhwch.html

Gwyndaf, R., (1991) *Fairylore: Memorates and Legends from Welsh Oral Tradition; The Good People*

Harms, D., Clark, J., and Peterson, J., (2015) *The Book of Oberon*

Harper, D., (2020) *Fairy.* Retrieved from https://www.etymonline.com/word/fairy

— (2020) *Elf*. Retrieved from https://www.etymonline.com/search?q=elf

Heath, C., (2021) *The Places We Go in Dream*. Retrieved from https://seohelrune.com/2021/02/16/the-places-we-go-in-dream/

Henderson, L., (1997) *The Guid Neighbours: Fairy Belief in Early Modern Scotland, 1500-1800*

— (2016) 'The (Super)natural world of Robert Kirk: Fairies, Beasts, Landscapes and Lychnobious Liminalities', *The Bottle Imp, Issue 20*

Henderson, L., and Cowan, E., (2007) *Scottish Fairy Belief*

Houlihan, M., (2022) *Irish Fairies: A Short History of the Sídhe*

Kirk, R., and Lang, R., (1893) *The Secret Commonwealth of Elves, Fauns, and Fairies*

Kruse, J., (2018) *Some Welsh Otherworlds*. Retrieved from https://britishfairies.wordpress.com/2018/08/12/some-welsh-otherworlds/

Larrington, C., (2006) *King Arthur's Enchantresses*

Laskaya, A., and Salisbury, E., (1995) *Sir Orfeo*

Lecouteux, C., (2003) *Witches, Werewolves, and Fairies: Shapeshifters and Astral Doubles in the Middle Ages*

Lindahl, C., McNamara, J., and Lindow, J., (2002) *Medieval Folklore: an encyclopaedia of myths, legends, tales, beliefs, and customs*

Lyle, E., (1970). *The Teind to Hell in Tam Lin*

MacKenzie, D., (1935) *Scottish Folk-lore and Folk Life*

MacKenzie, O., (1921) *A Hundred Years in the Highlands*

MacKillop, J., (1998) *Dictionary of Celtic Mythology*

MacNeill, M., (1962) *The Festival of Lughnasa*

Madden, F., (1847) *Layamon's Brut or Chronicles of Britain*. Retrieved from https://www.google.com/books/edition/Layamons_Brut_Or_Chronicle_of_Britain/1xAJAAAAQAAJ?hl=en

Mann, N., (2001) *The Isle of Avalon*

Matthews, J., (2004) *The Sidhe: Wisdom from the Celtic Otherworld*

McCone, K., (2000) *Pagan Past and Christian Present in Early Irish Literature*

McNeill, F., (1956) *The Silver Bough*

Morus-Baird, G., (2020) *The Celtic 'Otherworld'?* Retrieved from https://www.youtube.com/watch?v=Y5WiifupG-4

Murray, J., (1875) *The Romance and Prophecies of Thomas of Erceldoune*

— (1918) *The Romance and Prophecies of Thomas of Erceldoune*

— (1922) *The Complaynt of Scotland*

Narvaez, P., (1991) *The Good People: New Fairylore Essays*

Nutt, A., (1895) *The Voyage of Bran son of Febal to the Land of the Living*. Retrieved from http://www.maryjones.us/ctexts/branvoyage.html

O Crualaoich, G., (2003) *The Book of the Cailleach: Stories of the Wise-woman Healer*

— (2006) 'Reading the Bean Feasa', *Folklore, vol. 116*

Olsen, K., and Veenstra, J., (2014) *Airy Nothings: Imagining the Otherworld of Faerie from the Middle Ages to the Age of Reason*

Parry, J., (1925) *The Vita Merlini*

Pitcairn, R., (1833) *Ancient Criminal Trials in Scotland*

Plumtree, J., (2022) *Placing the Green Children of Woolpit*

Purkiss, D., (2000) *At the Bottom of the Garden: A Dark History of Fairies, Hobgoblins, and Other Troublesome Things*

Rhys, J., (1907) *Celtic Folklore Welsh and Manx*

Robertson, C., (1905) *Folk-lore from the West of Ross-shire*

Scott, W., (1802) *Minstrelsy of the Scottish Border: Consisting of Historical and Romantic Ballads, Collected in the Southern Counties of Scotland; With a Few of Modern Date, Founded Upon Local Tradition*

Shakespeare, W., (2004) *A Midsummer Night's Dream*

— (1974) *The Complete Works of William Shakespeare*

Silver, C., (1999) *Strange & Secret Peoples: Fairies and the Victorian Consciousness*

Sims-Williams, P., (2011) *Irish Influence on Medieval Welsh Literature*

Skene, W., (2007) '*The Dialogue of Gwyddno Garanhir and Gwyn ap Nudd,*' *The Four Ancient Books of Wales*

Smithers, L., (2014) *Gwynn ap Nudd and the Spirits of Annwn*. Retrieved from https://lornasmithers.wordpress.com/2014/07/31/gwyn-ap-nudd-and-the-spirits-of-annwn-remembering-the-underworld-gods/

Spangler, D., (2014) *Conversations with the Sidhe*

Spyra, P., (2015) *The Terrors of the Threshold: Liminality and the Fairies of Sir Orfeo*. https://www.academia.edu/32227889/The_Terror_of_the_Threshold_Liminality_and_the_Fairies_of_Sir_Orfeo

— (2020) *The Liminality of Fairies: Readings in Late Medieval English and Scottish Romance*

Stokes, W., (1862) *Three Irish Glossaries: Cormac's glossary codex A, O'Davoren's glossary, and a glossary to the calendar of Oingus the Culdee*. Retrieved from https://archive.org/details/cu31924026508238

Thorpe, L., (2021) *Gerald of Wales: Two Accounts of the Exhumation of Arthur's Body*. Retrieved from https://web.archive.org/web/20130918052525/http://www.britannia.com/history/docs/debarri.html

Twomey, M., (2008) '*Morgan la Fey, Empress of the Wilderness*'., Retrieved from https://www.academia.edu/11688947

Wade, J., (2011) *Fairies in Medieval Romance*

Walsh, B., (2002). *The Secret Commonwealth and the Fairy Belief Complex*

Weston, J., (1914) *The Chief Middle English Poets*

Wilby, E., (2005) *Cunning Folk and Familiar Spirits: Shamanistic Visionary Traditions in Early Modern British Witchcraft and Magic*

— (2010) *The Visions of Isobel Gowdie: Magic, Witchcraft, and Dark Shamanism in Seventeenth Century Scotland*

Wilde, E., (1888) *Ancient Legends, Mystic Charms, and Legends of Ireland*

Williams Ab Ithel, J., (1836) *The Barddas of Iolo Morganwg, vol 1 & 2*

Williams, M., (2016) *Ireland's Immortals*

Williams, N., (1991) *The Semantics of the Word Fairy: Making Meaning Out of Thin Air; The Good People*

Wooding, J., (2000) *The Otherworld Journey in Early Irish Literature*

Young, S., (2022) *Dark Thoughts on the Wollaton Gnomes*. Retrieved from http://www.strangehistory.net/2022/01/31/dark-thoughts-on-the-wollaton-gnomes/

— (2018*) Fairy Census*. Retrieved from http://www.fairyist.com/wp-content/uploads/2014/10/The-Fairy-Census-2014-2017-1.pdf

About the Author

Morgan Daimler is a blogger, poet, teacher of esoteric subjects, witch, and priestess of the Daoine Maithe. Morgan is a prolific pagan writer, having published more than a dozen books under Moon Books alone, and she is one of the world's foremost experts on all things Fairy. She lives in Connecticut, USA.

SELECTED TITLES

Norse Mythology
Odin

Thor

Freya

The Norse

Fairy Lore
Fairies

Fairycraft

Aos Sidhe

Fairy Witchcraft

21st Century Fairy

A New Dictionary of Fairies

Irish Mythology
Lugh

The Dagda

The Morrigan

Irish Paganism

Raven Goddess

Manannán mac Lir

You may also like

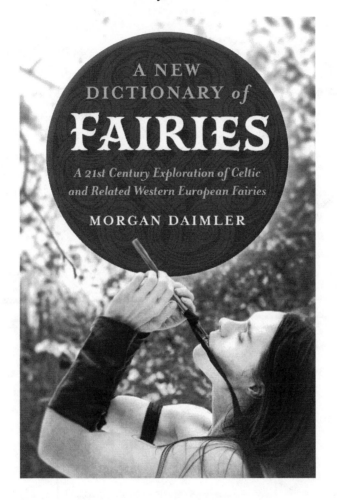

A New Dictionary of Fairies
*A 21ˢᵗ Century Exploration of Celtic
and Related Western European Fairies*
Morgan Daimler

978-1-78904-036-4 (Paperback)
978-1-78904-037-1 (e-book)

Bestsellers from Moon Books

Keeping Her Keys
An Introduction to Hekate's Modern Witchcraft
Cyndi Brannen
*Blending Hekate, witchcraft and personal
development together to create
a powerful new magickal perspective.*
Paperback: 978-1-78904-075-3 ebook 978-1-78904-076-0

Journey to the Dark Goddess
How to Return to Your Soul
Jane Meredith
*Discover the powerful secrets of the Dark Goddess and
transform your depression, grief and pain into healing
and integration.*
Paperback: 978-1-84694-677-6 ebook: 978-1-78099-223-5

Shamanic Reiki
Expanded Ways of Working with Universal Life Force Energy
Llyn Roberts, Robert Levy
*Shamanism and Reiki are each powerful ways of healing; together,
their power multiplies. Shamanic Reiki introduces techniques to
help healers and Reiki practitioners tap ancient healing wisdom.*
Paperback: 978-1-84694-037-8 ebook: 978-1-84694-650-9

Southern Cunning
Folkloric Witchcraft in the American South
Aaron Oberon
*Modern witchcraft with a Southern flair, this book is a
journey through the folklore of the American South and
a look at the power these stories hold for modern witches.*
Paperback: 978-1-78904-196-5 ebook: 978-1-78904-197-2

Readers of ebooks can buy or view any of these bestsellers by clicking on the live link in the title. Most titles are published in paperback and as an ebook. Paperbacks are available in traditional bookshops. Both print and ebook formats are available online.

Find more titles and sign up to our readers' newsletter
http://www.johnhuntpublishing.com/paganism

For video content, author interviews and more, please subscribe to our YouTube channel.

MoonBooksPublishing

Follow us on social media for book news, promotions and more:

Facebook: Moon Books Publishing

Instagram: @moonbooksjhp

Twitter: @MoonBooksJHP

Tik Tok: @moonbooksjhp